SALVATION BY SURPRISE

Salvation by Surprise

*A Commentary on
the Book of Romans*

Earl F. Palmer

REGENT COLLEGE PUBLISHING
VANCOUVER, CANADA

For my family:
Shirley
Anne, 13
Jonathan, 9
Elizabeth, 5

Contents

Preface

For a long time I have wanted to write down my own reflections on Paul's letter to the Romans. From the early beginnings of my own Christian life, this New Testament book has deeply etched its influence upon my thinking and my faith, and by God's grace upon my life. As a pastor in Seattle, then Manila, and now in Berkeley, I have thought, taught, and wondered about this letter more than any other in the Bible. Now this study comes into print, fulfilling my own long-standing desire to present a commentary which I hope will also become a guide to Christians and non-Christians alike—enabling a thorough study of Romans, and indeed the Christian faith as well.

No other book in the New Testament has had the theological influence of Paul's brief letter to his brothers and sisters in Rome, and no other book has earned as many commentaries in the history of New Testament scholarship. I believe that its shattering, healing message deserves yet another interpretation. My goal in this study is to establish a linkage between our generation in this latter half of the twentieth century, and the timeless words of Paul at the midpoint of his century.

I want to thank the many friends who helped me to write this study; the congregation of First Presbyterian Church of Berkeley; Tyndale House, Cambridge, England; Arba Hudgens for his wise counsel, Dale Bruner who has encouraged me to write; my mother and father who have encouraged me every step of the way; and my secretary, Miss Dorothy Gilroy. It has been Shirley my wife who has helped me most of all, and not only in this project.

EARL PALMER
Berkeley, California

Introduction

Paul is the writer of this New Testament book. He was formerly Saul of Tarsus, a man gifted with the rich background of Greek cultural education and Jewish tradition. Tarsus was the city where Stoicism's founder Zeno had lived, and it also boasted one of the greatest libraries in the first-century world.

As we examine the life of Paul, we realize that he understands and feels at home in the culture of Greek civilization. He is a Roman citizen as well. But the Paul we meet in Romans is a son of Israel too. He claims his personal ancestry to the tribe of David, and is a member of the Pharisee party—a lay movement stretching back to the time of the Maccabean Revolt. Pharisaism had developed a brave nationalistic tradition devoted to the law and the traditions of Israel. But Paul writes his letter to Rome for a more important reason than his enlightenment in classical Greek thought or his involvement in the Pharisee movement. Why? Because in the middle of his life he met and believed in Jesus. It is now this new Paul, the messenger of Jesus Christ, who writes to the church at Rome.

The letter to the Romans is Paul's major work. It has challenged Christians through the centuries and has played a key role in each of the great periods of renewal and reformation of the church. The letter is written with precision—more so than the spontaneous Galatians, Philippians, and 1 and 2 Corinthians. It covers more subjects in more depth than the shorter books of 1 and 2 Thessalonians, Philemon, Titus, and 1 and 2 Timothy. It is not as devotional and personal as Philippians or Philemon. Colossians, Galatians and Ephesians are similar to Romans because of their theological style, and they tend to complement this book, further enlarging areas of doctrine which the Roman letter introduces. But they lack the overall sweep of this letter.

Though Romans is more formally constructed than Paul's other letters, this is not to imply that the Apostle has, therefore, covered all Christian doctrines within the sixteen chapters. There are many Christian themes that are not fully discussed by Paul within this letter, and some issues not dealt with at all. He has limited the scope, though the themes he has chosen are tremendously significant for any person who wants seriously to face up to the meaning of the Christian faith for his or her own life. Each theme within the book is interrelated. Bruce Metzger writes:

> The content of Romans was not the flash of the moment writing, but had been maturing in Paul's thinking and teaching over many years. Therefore, what he sets forth in one part of the letter cannot be isolated from what he has said or is going to say in another part.[1]

Dr. Metzger's counsel is vital for the reader of this letter. We must read and understand Romans in its total context because the whole of the book sets up and preserves the significance of the parts.

The textual controversies with regard to Romans are relatively uncomplicated. Some commentators see the final greeting (16:25-27) as a later addition or perhaps a chapter from another Pauline book in view of the greeting already present in 15:30–33 and 16:20. Rudolph Bultmann has hypothesized, however without manuscript support, that a selection of verses in chapter 8, as well as 3:24–25, were glosses to the book. In spite of these textual questions, the book as it stands in the rsv text has held its ground and enjoys the most secure critical position of all New Testament books.

The date of Romans is difficult to fix with certainty, though the most recent scholarly consensus places the date of writing at or around 47 A.D. and the place of writing as Corinth.

The question of the relationship of Romans and Paul himself to the contemporary philosophical, theological, and religious setting of his time is a question which this commentary will seek to meet as we look at specific passages in the letter itself. It is important continually to ask, What exactly is the ideological climate within which Paul writes? Is Paul's writing influenced primarily by the "gospel of God" (1:1), or is that good news incorporated by Paul into a synthesis of philosophical influences that have their origin elsewhere? Is Paul's portrayal of Jesus Christ essentially the same as in the narratives of Matthew, Mark, and Luke? What is the relationship between Paul and John's Gospel? There are debates among New Testament scholars that have centered upon these issues, and answers to such questions resolve best as the literature of Paul is compared point by point with the narratives of the Gospels and Acts, as well as the non-Pauline New Testament books.

Luke tells us that the church at Jerusalem accepted the gospel that Paul taught (Acts 15) and accepted his mission to the Greek world. It will be my contention that Romans is the key link in the evidence that establishes Paul's conscious agreement with the apostolic church concerning the nature and essential message of the "gospel of God" (both Paul's phrase and Mark's). See Mark 1:14. I believe that one of Paul's purposes in this letter is to firmly establish the crucial unity of his message with the message of the Christians at

Jerusalem and the apostles. For this reason, in my judgment, Paul will make use of parts of four apostolic church credal statements throughout the book which he intentionally incorporates into his own argument, and then follows with his own comments in order to make the united affirmation of the early church clear to the Romans. It is possible that these four credal formulas were known, understood, and recited by the Roman church as part of the gospel of Jesus Christ that had already been preached to them and in which they already believed. The four credal formulas come at strategic places within the letter: 1:2–4; 3:24–25; 10:9–10; and 16:25–26.[2]

If, in fact, Paul's letter can be understood as a conscious enlargement upon these very early affirmations of the apostolic church, we then possess within Romans our most important first-century document in the dialogue of the early church as to the meaning of the gospel of Jesus Christ. It is my view that such is the case and that Romans is Paul's thoughtful contribution to that unity. The Apostle also grapples within this letter with two difficult issues that the very early Christian church was forced to encounter: *legalism*, rooted in the pervasive influence of the church's Jewish heritage, and an *incipient gnosticism* rooted in the constant pressure and influence of four centuries of Greek philosophical and mythological outlook within the Greek world. The primary pastoral concern of the Apostle Paul is to encourage the Christian to obey the truth of the gospel in all of life so that in the face of the real world they may not only survive, but become a part of changing the world through the gospel of Jesus Christ.

There remains one further point to which I would like to refer, and that concerns the *authority* of the Book of Romans, and along with it the Bible as a whole—Old and New Testaments. The Bible gains its authority in borrowed fashion from its center Jesus Christ. It is the Jesus Christ of the Bible who wins us to himself and through him we are bound by the Holy Spirit to the book that bears witness to him. This means that all Christian doctrine and affirmation must be obedient to the witness of the Bible; that is, we are to test our doctrines and our lives by the faithful witness to Jesus Christ which is what the Bible is: the Old Testament is anticipation and the New Testament is fulfillment. The church's doctrine of inspiration means that the biblical documents are the faithful witness of God's self evidence by the Holy Spirit, and that therefore they are authoritative for us, the unfallible rule for faith and life. It is the book that God wants us to have, and on the basis of its teaching we are called to the task of sharing its living center, Jesus Christ, to our own age. This binding of our life to the biblical witness is what in fact sets us free from the recurring cycles of cultism, the dreams and visions of powerful people around us who desire to create doctrine on the basis of their own experience. As Christians, we are thankful for experiences but we do not build doctrines from them, nor are we to draw up movements on the basis of any test but the test of the witness of the Holy Scripture. Where the church remembers its obedience to the biblical witness it is most relevant to the world.

Part 1

Credo

> 1: 1)Paul, a servant of Jesus Christ, called to be an apostle, set apart for the gospel of God 2)which he promised beforehand through his prophets in the holy scriptures, 3)the gospel concerning his Son, who was descended from David according to the flesh 4)and designated Son of God in power according to the Spirit of holiness by his resurrection from the dead, Jesus Christ our Lord, 5)through whom we have received grace and apostleship to bring about the obedience of faith for the sake of his name among all the nations, 6)including yourselves who are called to belong to Jesus Christ.

Paul's opening greeting to the Romans is similar to those in other letters, yet it is notably longer and more complex. In verses 2–4 there appears a statement about the gospel of God which may be described as a credal formula, a statement of faith. The question then is this: Is Paul the initiator of this statement, or is he incorporating into his greeting something that the Christians at Rome already know, have already heard, perhaps memorized, and even used in their worship and witness? First, let us sketch in the main ingredients of the statement. (1) The formula affirms the witness to Christ by the Old Testament Scriptures. (2) The formula claims that Jesus Christ is the true center of the gospel of God. (3) The formula affirms that Jesus is God's son, heir of David, fulfillment of the prophet's expectation, the one confirmed by the Holy Spirit through his actual victory over death.

Verse 5 may be the point where Paul begins his reflection upon the statement of faith. His conclusion is that through this very Jesus Christ comes the gracious call to the Roman Christians, and all people everywhere, to obey the Lordship of God's son.

The statement of faith in this passage sounds much like a similar affirmation in Peter's sermon on the Day of Pentecost (Acts 2:22–28). Peter also makes use of the word used here *oridzo* (translated "designate"). He also employs that word to describe the true deity of Jesus Christ. Paul again uses the word in his sermon at Mars Hill (Acts 17:31). I believe C. H. Dodd is correct in treating this statement as a credal formula with which the Christians at Rome are already familiar.[1] Perhaps Paul quotes the brief credo at the opening of his letter so that he 'might achieve two goals: (1) He makes clear his own agreement with the faith of the Christians at Jerusalem and Rome. Paul is not preaching a new gospel but the very gospel to which Peter, James, and John have also pledged their lives. In this way Paul demonstrates concretely at the opening of the letter his own solidarity with the whole first-century church as to that which is rightly central—Jesus Christ the Lord. (2) The Apostle intends to describe his own experiences of what the implications of that gospel are to him in everyday life.

At the opening of the letter, then, the Apostle Paul does not fully explain the affirmation but rather states it and then calls the reader to the obedience and Lordship of Christ.

"It is not, however, his present purpose to expound his theology, but to place on record the facts which he and his Roman readers alike regarded as fundamental," says C. H. Dodd. There is a serious question in this opening statement as to whether Paul is preaching adoptionism. Paul's use of the word "designate" has been a source of debate on this issue because of a misunderstanding of the theological content.

> The exegetical dispute whether Romans 1:4 according to usage attested elsewhere is a declaration or decree concerning Christ, or his appointment and institution to a function or relation is not a matter of great urgency, since a divine declaration is the same as a divine appointment: God's *verbum* is *efficax.* But behind the dispute there is an important point . . . the appointment of Jesus (Christ) as what he is to be must be equated with what he already is from the very beginning of the world, from all eternity in God's decree.[2]

By no means, then, is the Apostle intending to teach the adoptionist doctrine that Jesus at some point in his life is adopted to sonship; rather, that Jesus of Nazareth (at the Jordan River before baptism) is *already* the very Speech of God breaking through. The witness of the Holy Spirit following that baptism (Luke 3:21–22) does not, therefore, make Jesus the Lord but rather attests to Jesus as Lord.

Paul's greeting closes with the sentence that is his own unique autograph in every letter. "Grace to you and peace from God our Father and the Lord Jesus Christ." The full wording may vary from letter to letter, though the words *grace* and *peace* always appear.

Why does he use these words? Paul's intent may be to unite two great words from two great traditions: the Jewish *shalom* "peace" and the Greek *charis* "grace." With these words he combines the aspirations of two cultural traditions and unites them together in their dependence upon God our Father and the Lord Jesus Christ. Paul has consciously combined Greek and Jewish longings for *wholeness* and *fulfillment;* he claims that each longing is found and fulfilled in Jesus Christ.

8)First, I thank my God through Jesus Christ for all
of you, because your faith is proclaimed in all the
world. 9)For God is my witness, whom I serve with
my spirit in the gospel of his Son, that without ceasing
I mention you always in my prayers, 10) asking that
somehow by God's will I may now at last succeed in
coming to you. 11)For I long to see you, that I may
impart to you some spiritual gift to strengthen you,
12)that is, that we may be mutually encouraged by
each other's faith, both yours and mine. 13) I want
you to know, brethren, that I have often intended to
come to you (but thus far have been prevented), in
order that I may reap some harvest among you as well
as among the rest of the Gentiles. 14) I am under obligation both to Greeks and to barbarians, both to the
wise and to the foolish: 15) so I am eager to preach
the gospel to you also who are in Rome.

This third paragraph of the letter contains Paul's prayer of
thanksgiving for the Christians at Rome; it is in this prayer
context that the Apostle announces his plan to travel to
Rome in order to share his own mission with the Christians
there and to receive the gift of their life in faith to him.

The word *barbarios* "barbarian" is used by Paul in its first-
century technical sense to describe those who were not
among the Greek-speaking part of the first-century world.
Note that in several dramatic ways the Apostle Paul has
claimed for the gospel its universal relevance: by the use of
the words *ethnos* and *barbarios;* also the words wise, foolish,
grace, peace, Jews and Greeks.

The Apostle has stirred up his reader's interest in themes
and subjects which shall now become the purpose of his
letter.

Part 2

The Credibility Question

> 16)For I am not ashamed of the gospel: it is the power
> of God for salvation to every one who has faith, to the
> Jew first and also to the Greek. 17)For in it the right-
> eousness of God is revealed through faith for faith;
> as it is written, "He who through faith is righteous
> shall live."

"I am not ashamed of the gospel, because I am convinced
of its universal relevancy." This is the force of these two
remarkable verses. Paul claims that the gospel is the powerful word from God for the whole world—Jew and Greek.
The very rescue and wholeness of the world depends upon
the breakthrough into human history of the character of
God.

The first 17 verses of Romans is the introduction to Paul's
entire letter. To put it another way, the Apostle Paul's credal
affirmation in 1:2–4 is to become the preface and thesis
statement that sets up his exposition form in the book as a
whole. In that opening statement, Paul has affirmed the following:

1) The centrality of Jesus Christ.
2) That this Jesus is the fulfillment of the Old
   Testament messianic expectation.

3) And thirdly, Paul has challenged his readers
to believe in the claim of Jesus Christ the Lord
upon our lives.

Note that Paul's message as set forth in 1:1–5 contains
the same overall structure and content as the Apostle Peter's
sermon at the Day of Pentecost (Acts 2:14–39): (1) the
centrality of the word and work of Jesus (Acts 2:22–24);
(2) the affirmation of Jesus as the fulfillment of Old Testament prophecy (Acts 2:17–21, 25–36); and (3) the challenge to the people to obey Christ's claim upon their lives
(Acts 2:37–39).

The question we must ask is this: When the early Christians preached their faith to inquirers during the period
between the resurrection of Jesus and the actual writing of
the New Testament documents (letters of Paul, and the
Gospels), what was it they said to the people? What was the
form and content of that earliest message of the church to
the world? We are maintaining that Paul's message, as recorded in his letters, is in full agreement with the preaching
(kerygma) of the early church as believed and preached by
Peter, John, Philip, Stephen, and now, by the year 47 A.D.,
believed and preached by a widely expanding company of
believers. We have speculated that Paul has very likely
incorporated commonly held statements of early church
faith at four strategic places within the letter (1:2–5; 3:24–
25; 10:9–10; 16:25–26). Perhaps in these places Paul may
even employ the exact wording of the early church language
of faith. This explains why words and sentence structure
appear in these four places which are not typical of Paul's
usual writing style. For example, Paul does not usually make
reference to King David. His preference is to call attention
to Abraham. The use of the word "mercy seat" in 3:24–25
is nowhere else mentioned by Paul. The very obvious Hebrew present in 10:9–10 is not typical of Paul.

Luke's record of Peter's sermon, Philip's witness to the

Ethiopian official, Stephen's witness, Paul's sermon at Athens, together with the synoptic records, enable us to draw some conclusions as to the nature of early church preaching. What, then, are the main ingredients of that preaching? Let us draw together the principal ingredients of the apostolic message.

First, the kerygma was Christocentric. Luke tells us that Philip's sermon to the Ethiopian official consisted of the following. "Then Philip opened his mouth, and beginning with this scripture [Isaiah 53], he [Philip] told him the good news of Jesus" (Acts 8:35). The largest part of apostolic preaching was spent in recounting the events of Jesus' life—Jesus said these things; he met the people; they asked questions of him; Jesus taught them; he prayed; he healed the sick; he set his face toward Jerusalem; he entered the city on the first day of the week of Passover; the people of Jerusalem recognized him as king; he shared the Last Supper with his disciples; he was arrested at Gethsemane; he was crucified; on the first day of the week he conquered death; he has won our obedience; in his name we preach; this Jesus will come again in final vindication of his reign. The Book of Acts contains compressed accounts of such narrative witnesses. (See Luke's single line statement regarding Philip's sermon.) The explanation of the greatly shortened reference by Luke is precisely because Luke has already written a longer Gospel record. *This means that the synoptic Gospel accounts are examples of early church preaching.* Peter, as he spoke on Pentecost Day, may have sounded much like the Book of Mark, unfolding scene after scene from the life of Jesus. Paul probably did the same at Mars Hill. The Christians told their contemporaries about the word and the work of Jesus—of what he did and said. This was the preaching of the early church.

Professor Rudolph Bultmann, in my judgment, has made a major error in his own quest for the "Easter faith" of primitive Christianity in failing to adequately recognize the profound indebtedness and linkage of Paul and the early church to the historical events of the life of Jesus. Jesus Christ is an actual event for them, just as surely as he is their eschatological hope and conviction. Paul, preaching the gospel to the philosophers at Athens, is speaking of the historical Jesus and of the actual victory over death by the actual Jesus of Nazareth. It is Dr. Bultmann's own student, Ernst Käsemann, who describes the dead-end street into which the Bultmannian school of biblical interpretation has trapped itself. Käsemann wonders, "Why were the Gospels written in the first place if the early church is so preoccupied with its own Easter faith and so little concerned with the narrative, scene by scene events that make up so large and exciting a part of the New Testament."[1]

"Who was descended from David . . ." (1:3). The second part of the kerygma of the early church is the claim that in Jesus himself is the fulfillment of the Old Testament's messianic longings.

This is also the case in Paul's credo of 1:3–6. The point is that both Peter and Paul press the claim that the Old Testament is fulfilled in Jesus Christ. What Paul states by a single phrase in chapter 1 will be developed in more depth later in the letter. We must now attempt to understand, therefore, the nature of the Old Testament expectation as it was felt by the first-century Jewish person. Within the Romans letter, Paul will gather together the threads of Old Testament expectation by his own strategic use of three Old Testament figures: David—1:2–5; Abraham—chapter 4; Moses and the Law—chapters 2 and 10. A diagram may be helpful in sketching these Old Testament threads of expectation.

One way to understand the history of Israel is in the perspective of these three Old Testament figures. It can be said that throughout the Old Testament journey, the people longed for a father like Abraham, an emancipator like Moses, a king like David. Those yearnings come into the first-century expectation of Israel too, now colored and influenced

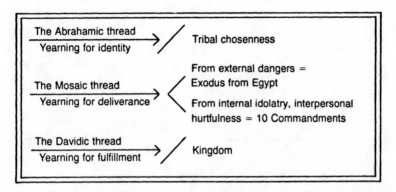

by the experiences of the people under many years of foreign domination (for practical terms since the year 710 B.C.).

Within the Old Testament literature these three threads have their own synthesis in the writings of the Old Testament prophets:

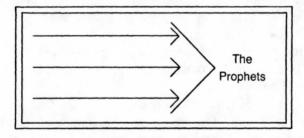

The prophets draw together the yearnings. It is the prophet who speaks in behalf of God over against the priesthood (Abrahamic thread) and the kings (Davidic) and the scribes of the Law (Mosaic); yet, at the same time, seeking the preservation of the true meaning of each vital thread for the people of God. The prophets achieve this synthesis by their own unique message in the name of God—the result is their message from God of *judgment* and *hope*.

The two prophetic words, the *yes* and the *no* of Almighty God are always present in the prophets and usually in the same textual setting. Both judgment and hope are portrayed

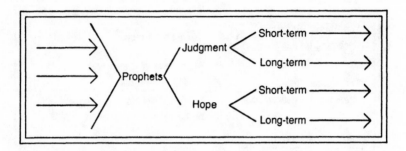

by the prophets in long-term and short-term perspectives. Judgment, short-term, refers to the leveling by God of the people and their institutions in an immediate sense. An example of this short-term judgment perspective is found in the words of Jeremiah against his people in the face of the neo-Babylonian forces encamped around Jerusalem (Jer. 30:12–16). Literally, within weeks Jerusalem is to be destroyed—of this judgment the Prophet Jeremiah writes oracle after oracle. But there is judgment in the Old Testament which is long-term, apocalyptic, and mysterious. Joel's obscure prediction of the moon turned to blood (Joel 2:28–32) is a prophetic passage in the Old Testament of this second form.

The word of hope is also portrayed by the Old Testament prophets in both time tenses as well, long-term/short-term. The short-term hope is the immediate promise to Israel and Judah that if the people will repent of their sins, then they may expect the forgiveness of God in an immediate sense (Isa. 1:16–18).

But as in the case of the judgment word of the prophets, there are the long-term words of hope which tell of the act of God beyond the immediate situation and which promise that God will himself be Savior as he also is Judge. Jeremiah 33:14–22 speaks of this hope, "For thus says the Lord: David shall never lack a man to sit on the throne. . . ."

The message of the New Testament in the face of these Old Testament threads, together with the prophetic hope and judgment, affirms that all longings and prophecies converge and are resolved, and find their fulfillment in God's mighty act: Jesus of Nazareth.

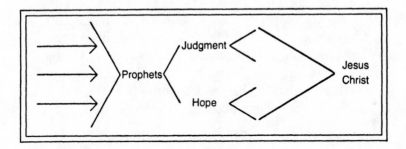

More than this, Paul will claim that the longings of all men, Greeks and Jews alike, are fulfilled in Christ—even those people who are without the signposts of the Old Testament to guide them. This is what he teaches at Athens (Acts 17). The eternal God is able to speak for himself, and God's speech fulfills the profoundest yearnings of all mankind, including even the most subtle aspirations of the Greek philosophers.

Paul goes further than indelibly sketching in this Christian premise (1:3-6, 16-17). He also claims that this gospel is *good* news; that it is *powerful;* that it salvages and makes safe; that it is righteous.[2] Finally, Paul quotes as his text the Old Testament prophetic sentence, Habakkuk 2:4.[3]

The broad appeal of this basic and forthright New Testament message about Jesus Christ is one of the indisputable facts of the first century. Therefore, when Paul writes to the Romans he is aware, from his own experience, of the strong and universal attraction of the person of Jesus upon *all* first-century persons. He saw it for himself in a Philippian jail, at Ephesus, at Corinth, at Antioch.[4]

In the early part of the second century a Roman official, Pliny the younger, will write to the Secretariat of the Emperor Trajan an official report concerning the Christian

movement in his province (Asia Minor). In his final paragraph Pliny gives us a fascinating clue to the incredible
spread of the Christian church:

> The matter seemed to me to justify my consult-
> ing you, especially on account of the number of
> those imperilled; for many persons of all ages and
> classes and of both sexes are being put in peril by
> accusation, and this will go on. The contagion of
> this superstition has spread not only in the cities,
> but in the villages and rural districts as well. . . .[5]

Today the appeal of Jesus of Nazareth continues to thrive
on the tests of fads and media. In the second half of the
twentieth century the question, *Who is Jesus Christ?* is as
vital a concern for Christian and non-Christian alike as it
was in the time of Pliny the younger.

> Standing before the cross then, our defenses are
> down. Our bluff is called. Our alternative pursuits
> collapse. There we may understand that all power
> is a sham, all splendor is thorns, all the stains and
> styles of greatness so much mockery. There we are
> made aware at last of our own nothingness—which
> God deigned to put on. Standing before the cross,
> God's purpose for us is blindingly clear, to love
> him, to love our neighbor, which means everyone
> without exception, so that we may be worthy
> members of a human family whose father is in
> heaven, so that we may participate in what St.
> Paul called the glorious liberty of the children of
> God, the only true liberty there is or ever can be.[6]

1:16 "Jews first . . ." In sheer percentages, the greatest
following of the gospel came from the Jewish nation of the
first century. The Jews were a family oriented people:
religious, nationalistic, economically underdeveloped, cultur-
ally rich. They did not enjoy the wealth or political power

of the Romans, or the intellectual sophistication of the Greeks who contributed the language and intellectual categories of the first-century world. Nevertheless, they possessed the amazingly complete treasury of their Old Testament and intertestamental literature and heritage. They knew who they were. The Jewish Christians, like Paul himself, were those who recognized that Jesus is the fulfillment to the quest and journey of Israel. Here is Abraham's identity fulfilled, the law completed and made concrete, and here is David's king. Here is the Father like Abraham, the Deliverer like Moses, the King like David. In short, those Jews who trusted in the gospel of Jesus Christ found in him the completion of the law and the prophets of the Old Testament.

But there were also many in Israel who did not believe. Jesus both fulfilled and disappointed the expectations of his listeners—usually at the same time. The New Testament accounts make no attempt to hide this fact. On the one hand there is something which draws his followers to him, and at the same moment causes others to decide against him. On Palm Sunday Jesus is the man for the masses, and yet he does not take advantage of his popular attractiveness to weld those very masses together as a political–social movement. There are no torchlight parades that first night of the week, because Jesus does not show interest in building "the movement." Rather, he slips away from his friends to the hillside town of Bethany and cannot be found by the people. Could this have been the final disappointment for Judas, the urban activist who is now totally frustrated by this strange leader who defies every definition and captivity, who cannot be managed even by his friends?

The fact is, one of the reasons Jesus is so unforgettable in the Gospel accounts is precisely because of the rich mixture of disappointment and fulfillment of the religious, philosophical, and cultural expectations of what the Messiah would or should be like. Certainly for first-century Jews who have tribal and messianic hopes mixed together, Jesus is not the answer they were looking for. We know from Luke that John the Baptist had in mind a Lord with fire in one hand and the axe of judgment in the other to clear the threshing floor once and for all. John was not really prepared for the Lamb of God who would resolve evil by taking upon himself that full and awesome judgment at Calvary. In one way or another something fulfills and bothers each one; the offense and the appeal continue through the ages. In our own ideological existential age, we, like John the Baptist, may favor revolutionary fire and axe, but at the same time we are somehow embarrassed and bothered by the Jesus who actually and concretely reaches out to touch the man with leprosy (Mark 1:40–45). It is not the sort of revolution we have in mind. Many twentieth-century readers reject the miracle events as historical narrations, and then wonder why early Christians sought to illustrate love in such simple, direct, concrete ways. Nevertheless, the Gospel records haunt us, and with every new manuscript discovery, the texts still stand; in fact, are more permanently etched in, as the years come and go. The miracles recorded in the Gospel records continue to embarrass every hermeneutical frame-work carefully established to exclude the particular, the definite acts of God. It is this unique and concrete Jesus Christ, the Lord who is the Word of God, that the gospel is about, and many in the family of Abraham, Moses, and David believed; others would not or were not able to ac-cept his claim.

1:16 "Also the Greek. . . ." The gospel won Greeks as well as Jews. The Greeks were the intellectuals of the first century. They tended to be cynical and disillusioned. Stoi-cism and Epicureanism were both 400 years old by the time of Paul, and in each case the excitement was almost gone out of the movements and decay had set in. Greek–Roman religion in the first century was confused, even chaotic, with so many city gods and graduated deities that cities even maintained "catch-all" shrines to provide for divine emanations that might have been overlooked.

The scene in the first century was, in some ways, similar to my own city, Berkeley, in the 1970s, with the confusing mix of sub-culture, movements, and general ideological adriftness. Fads and causes ascend with novelty and descend with exposure—"nothing stays put for us" (Pascal). The permanent reality is more a mood, a nervous reaction, than a philosophy—it is an all-devouring *cynicism*. This was the context of the first century: affluent commercial cities, mobile population, moral confusion, games for the rich, despair for the poor. Into these very cities Paul planted himself and his companions. Beginning with the synagogue, reaching out to inquisitive Greek observers and even into the prominent marketplaces, Paul shared the gospel of the love of God.

We ask the question: What was it that convinced Greeks to become Christians? I believe one exciting part of the answer is revealed in the opening sentences of Paul's address on Mars Hill, "The God who made the world and everything in it, being Lord of heaven and earth, does not live in shrines made by man" (Acts 17:24). Paul rejects the various confinements of incipient Gnostic dualism (one god or set of gods for creation and a redeemer god for redemption).[7] He rejects the trivial and chaotic religious situation. In the place of the randomness that Athens offers Paul tells of Almighty God who is able to speak for himself and is not contained by the categories of human thought or the shrines of human devotion and fear. It seems to me that what was most convincing to the Greek mind then and now is the sheer vastness of this claim of the gospel—its radical sweep and integrating realism. Paul tells the Corinthians, "The love of Christ holds me together . . ." (2 Cor. 5:14). Finally, here in Jesus Christ is the truth genuinely radical enough to make sense of the whole, to hold the parts together.

"When they heard of the resurrection, some mocked Paul

. . ." (Acts 17:32). Ironically the Greek mind is impressed
by the vastness and totality of the Christian affirmation.
However, when that completeness is extended all the way,
even down into the wholeness and physical reality of history,
then resistance develops. The first-century Greek intellectual
may be eager to welcome the exciting spiritual dimensions
of the Christ, but because of his own bias against that which
is material and physical—both as seen in man the creature
and the physical world—he cannot easily welcome the
humiliation of God, which in the New Testament affirmation
is an integral part of the immensity of God. Father Murphy-
O'Connor points out that truth in the biblical sense, "can be
fully appreciated only within the framework of an historical
event, the covenant . . . is not an intellectual category but
a moral one . . . truth bears reference to activity, not
speculation. It is to be done and not merely to be contem-
plated." The Greek wants to honor Christ as a spiritual
force, but he is offended at the humiliated Christ who has
shown in the events of Good Friday and Easter a greatness
infinitely more sweeping than the spiritual ecstasies of eros.
At the cross of Christ we discover that the "omnipotence and
the grace of God are the same thing" (Karl Barth), but how
hard it is for the Greek philosopher to accept this new kind of
immensity. Plato is only willing to ascribe truth to pure
ideas, since for him the earth and all concreteness in history
is only apparent reality, a shadow of spiritual reality.

The Greek is therefore confronted, as is the Jew, each
in unique ways, with the gospel of Jesus Christ—stumbling
block and foolishness, yet strong and wise. The radicalness
and totality of the claim concerning Jesus Christ is new—
unforgettably new. A storm builds up around that proclamation and around the people of the proclamation too. The
church grows; the impressive fact is that the church grows
among all kinds of people; the gospel radically challenges
every expectation, yet the family of faith springs up.

Verses 16 and 17 close with Paul's repetitious use of the

word "faith." Faith, *pistis*, is the Greek word used in the Septuagint to translate the Hebrew word *Amen*—faithful, foundation rock, trustworthy. The word, therefore, because of its Old Testament meaning, may be used in two ways: to refer to man's faith and/or God's faithfulness. The context of the sentence always must guide the interpreter in establishing the correct definition. What is clear within the first seventeen verses of Romans is that the words "faith" and "faithfulness" are crucial to Paul. As the letter unfolds, the apostle will develop his definition of the word that is here only stated, and we must wait for the letter to establish its full meaning. What is clear to the reader by verse 17 is that faith, whatever the word means, is vital for the salvation of mankind.

Part 3

Cumulative Crises

Section 1—Romans 1:18–32

1: 18)For the wrath of God is revealed from heaven against all ungodliness and wickedness of men who by their wickedness suppress the truth. 19)For what can be known about God is plain to them, because God has shown it to them. 20)Ever since the creation of the world his invisible nature, namely, his eternal power and deity, has been clearly perceived in the things that have been made. So they are without excuse; 21) for although they knew God they did not honor him as God or give thanks to him, but they became futile in their thinking and their senseless minds were darkened. 22)Claiming to be wise, they became fools, 23) and exchanged the glory of the immortal God for images resembling mortal man or birds or animals or reptiles.

24)Therefore God gave them up in the lusts of their hearts to impurity, to the dishonoring of their bodies among themselves, 25) because they exchanged the truth about God for a lie and worshiped and served the creature rather than the Creator, who is blessed for ever! Amen. 26)For this reason God gave them up to dishonorable passions. Their women exchanged natural relations for unnatural, 27)and the men likewise gave up natural relations with women and were consumed with passion for one another, men committing shameless acts with men and receiving in their own persons the due penalty for their error.

28)And since they did not see fit to acknowledge
God, God gave them up to a base mind and to im-
proper conduct. 29)They were filled with all manner
of wickedness, evil, covetousness, malice. Full of envy,
murder, strife, deceit, malignity, they are gossips, 30)
slanderers, haters of God, insolent, haughty, boastful,
inventors of evil, disobedient to parents, 31)foolish,
faithless, heartless, ruthless. 32)Though they know
God's decree that those who do such things deserve
to die, they not only do them but approve those who
practice them.

"Paul's theology is always carefully thought out. The last
adjective one could apply to it would be 'naive.' "[1] The
book's first major section begins as if the author were an
Amos or John the Baptist, pacing back and forth within a
great universal courtroom. In 1:18–3:20, Paul the prosecutor is speaking and the case against the accused is carefully
established line upon line. Then suddenly, in 3:21 the
prosecutor crosses the room and speaks as the defense attorney.[2]

The fact is that the great defense of 3:21–5:21 needs the
foundation of this opening prosecution if it is to make sense.
Paul writes in the first major part of the book (1:18–3:20)
as an accuser of mankind; his style is not defensive or
apologetic. "The intention of the Apostle is not to infer
God's being from the world, but to uncover the being of the
world from God's revelation."[3] This strong and definitive
stance of the Apostle Paul in the opening pages makes the
book difficult for some readers to appreciate or to welcome.
But two facts about the harsh, brooding, negative thesis are
profoundly persuasive when the section is seriously read as
a whole: first, it is in the crucible of this very prosecution
section that Paul's whole view of man begins to take its
shape; second, we realize that for the first time in the history
of philosophy, a genuinely whole view of man is being put
together. Here at last is an understanding of the human
being without escapism, without spiritualization, and without cynicism. The view is really positive in the deepest sense

because it will be to a realistically understood human man and woman to whom the word of hope, beginning in 3:21, is addressed.

In these opening sentences, Paul faces squarely the chaos and the wholescale crisis of universal man—barbarians, Greeks, Jews.

In the intensity of his prosecution Paul never loses sight of the importance and value of man himself. Though men and women are guilty of sin, in deep trouble with God, each other, and the earth, nevertheless, the human being never becomes a worm or an object of contempt. In fact, the *freedom* of man which the Apostle insists upon and which becomes, in his polemic, a principal ingredient in the crisis —"although they knew . . . they did not" (1:21); "claiming to be wise" (1:22)—this very freedom is at the same moment the raw ingredient of greatness as much as it also is the ingredient of tragedy. Paul will later appeal to this freedom in building his theology of faith, hope, and love.

There are three primary themes that form the core of Paul's accusation in this passage (1:18–3:20). First he discusses the *origin of the human crisis;* second, the *cumulative nature of that crisis;* third, *the failure of every solution on man's part to find an adequate resolution to that crisis.*

1:18–23. First, Paul sketches in with a few bold sentences the origin of the human crisis. His affirmation is this: The tragedy of mankind consists in the breakdown and/or distortion of the vital relationships of man. He points out three relationships in these verses (1:18–32).

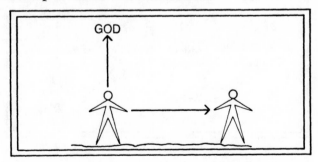

(1) The relationship with God, who is Creator (1:20), immortal (1:23), the author of truth (1:25)—this is the primary relationship for man. That is to say, in Paul's view, a human being must be related rightly to the Creator to be fully human.

When this primary relationship is broken by hostility toward God, the result for mankind is idolatry—"images resembling mortal man, birds, animals, reptiles." He calls it an "exchange." This is an historical observation on Paul's part; man is viewed by Paul as by nature religious, and he asks the reader to ponder this with him. In order to fill the void that results when God himself, the Creator and true source, is not the vital relationship of life, man inevitably seizes hold of other images (*aikon* is the word) to complete or fill up the void. As Paul lists the *aikons*, he alarms us by listing man as the first of the false gods, though man as a substitute for God soon gives way to a list of other "no gods."

"Whenever the qualitative distinction between men and the final omega is overlooked or misunderstood, that fetishism is bound to appear in which God is seen in birds or fourfooted things . . . family, nation, state, church, fatherland. And so the 'no god' is set up, idols are erected, and God, who dwells beyond all this and that, is given up."[4]

In Paul's portrayal there is a shift, a deterioration, in the idols that are chosen.

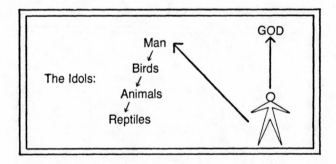

Note tne striking similarity between Romans 1:18–23 and the Book of Wisdom chapter 13.[5] Here, Paul makes use of some of the same arguments as does the Jewish writer of the Book of Wisdom, which was written in Alexandria in the Greek language somewhere in the second century B.C.[6] Note the portrayal of exchange whereby man in his foolishness turns away from the true God to images of his own creation. Note also the restlessness of idol worship—first one image, then another.

> Chapter 13:1. Surely vain are all men by nature, who are ignorant of God, and could not of the good things that are seen know him that is: neither by considering the works did they acknowledge the work master; but deemed either fire, or wind, or the swift air, or the circle of the stars, or the violent water, or the lights of heaven, to be the Gods which govern the world. . . .
>
> But miserable are they, and in dead things is their hope, who called them gods, which are the works of men's hands, gold and silver, to shew art in, and resemblances of beasts . . . and when he had nothing else to do, and formed it by the skill of his understanding, and fashioned it to the image of man . . . then maketh he prayer for his goods, for his wife and children, and is not ashamed to speak to that which hath no life. For health he calleth upon that which is weak, for life prayeth to that which is dead . . . and for gaining and getting; and for good success of his hands, asketh ability to do of him, that is most unable to do anything.

Paul's argument continues. The false worship of idols sooner or later gives way—collapses. The leader upon whom hopes were founded finally proves incapable of fulfilling his

followers' devotion. No person can sustain high homage for
long, so the followers are compelled to shift loyalties, and
now begins the endless wandering in search of adequate
aikons. The move is from no god to no god, from fad to fad,
from man to birds, from nations to family, from things to
four-footed creatures, and finally, in Paul's list, the reptiles—
that is, the worship of fear itself. Finally that which is
despised is honored in some futile hope, like Faust, to strike
a bargain with despair.

(2) In verses 24–26, the Apostle reviews his thesis and
then discusses the second relationship—man's self-understanding, his relationship with himself. It was Sigmund
Freud who theorized that the most important clue to a man
or woman's self-integration is found in the resolution or lack
of resolution of the individual's sexual nature within the
whole personality. Paul writes long before the psychoanalyt-
ical schools, but he chooses, in verses 1:26, 27, to describe
in general terms the confusion of men and women when they
have broken away from God. He describes that confusion
in this text by the use of sexual categories. This is not to
imply that sexual confusion is any more serious than the
chaos of other manifestations of the crisis, but sexual dis-
orientation is in Paul's argument a sign of the person who
does not know who he is in the light of God. Homosexuality
is not a major theme in Paul's writings,[7] but here he briefly
mentions homosexual men and women in this context to
explain the second stage of the human crisis. The human
being in broken relationship with the Creator finds his
identity confused; false *aikons* always cause a blurring of
self-understanding.

Paul employs lonely language in these self-awareness
sentences, "God gave them up to their own desires" (1:26),
and "receiving in their own persons" (1:27). "The enterprise
of setting up the 'no god' is avenged by its success . . . our
conduct becomes governed precisely by what we desire."[8]
This is the raw material of tragedy: that people chose idols

precisely in order to insure acceptance, power, success, and happiness. But in Paul's historical overview, every object of worship that we cling to for meaning will at the last spiral inwardly to the isolated results that verses 1:24–27 describe. C. S. Lewis in his book *The Great Divorce* characterizes hell as that state of being where each person lives an infinite distance from every other person. Our sins and our idols have done this to us.

The judgment language in 1:18–28 has the ring of finality about it—especially the threefold use of the phrase "God gave them up" (1:24, 26, 28). The verb is the same word used in Stephen's sermon recorded in Acts, "God gave them over" (Acts 7:42), and with reference to man himself Paul uses the verb in Ephesians 4:19, "They became callous and have given themselves up to licentiousness." Lightfoot[9] sees the use of this word as the "second stage in the downward fall of man," whereby it is God's judgment that man experience the effects in life of the moral law of a moral universe at work. The principal theological question then becomes, "How final is this giving up by God?" How ultimate, how complete is this act of divine judgment? If this passage (1:18–32) were allowed to stand alone then the prospects would appear grim and final. But the critical point to remember is that these harsh words do not stand apart from the whole of the book. John Calvin notes the intrinsic relatedness of Paul's words of judgment to the words of hope. The first must precede the second:

> . . . Paul's object is to teach us where salvation is to be found. He has already declared that we cannot obtain it except through the Gospel: but as the flesh will not willingly humble itself . . . Paul shows that the whole world is deserving of eternal death. It hence follows that life is to be recovered in some other way, since we are all lost in ourselves.[10]

Martin Luther also sees beyond the phrase "God gave them up" to the long-term purpose of God the Shepherd, " 'Therefore, God gave them up' . . . not only to let them have their way but also to teach them a lesson."[11]

Notice the marked similarity in 1:18–23, not only to the Book of Wisdom, but also to prophetic judgment literature throughout the Bible. There is also a finality expressed in Old and New Testament judgment language that intensifies the crisis to the point where there is no possibility of resolution apart from the mighty act of God himself.

Compare the following examples of Old and New Testament judgment passages: "Your hurt is incurable . . . there is none to uphold your cause, no medicine for your wound, no healing for you . . . because your guilt is great" (Jer. 30:12). Yet only eleven lines later in that very text, the Lord speaks through his prophet: "For I will restore health to you, and your wounds I will heal, says the Lord" (Jer. 30:17).

The letter to the seventh church in Revelation 3:14–22 contains the same mixture of overwhelming judgment followed by the surprising possibility of hope: "So, because you are lukewarm, and neither cold nor hot, I will spit you out of my mouth . . . Those whom I love, I reprove and chasten; so be zealous and repent. Behold I stand at the door and knock; if any one hears . . ."

Paul makes use of "gave them up" in the same prophetic sense as in the passages. "He gave them up" is the "next to the last word" that must be heard and experienced before "the last word" (Bonhoeffer) can really be heard.

> . . . It is only when one submits to the law that one can speak of grace, and only when one sees the anger and wrath of God hanging like grim realities over the head of one's enemies that one can know something of what it means to love them and forgive them. I don't think it is Christian to want to get to the New Testament too soon and

too directly. We have often talked about this before, and I am more than ever convinced that I am
right. You cannot and must not speak the last word
before you have spoken the next to last.[12]

(3) In 1:28–32 Paul turns the reader's attention to the
third vital relationship: the relationship of a man or woman
to the rest of the created order.

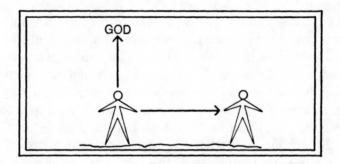

Paul's style is the same here as in the previous two parts
of the thesis, so the argument is sweeping. Idolatry results
in broken and hurtful human relationships. The long list of
sins in verses 29–32 is an attempt by Paul to point up the
complexity of hurtfulness and to bear witness to the terrify-
ing reality of man's crisis. He displays just a few of the
hundreds of possible words in the Greek language that
describe the harming results in life-to-life encounters of
the break with the true God and the subsequent loss of
identity.

Paul is not the only New Testament source for this theological interpretation of the ethical hurtfulness of idolatry.
In the Book of Revelation the relationship between idolatry
and immorality is also noted in the letters to Pergamos and
Thyatira (Rev. 2:12–29). Paul makes the connection firm
and unmistakable also in Colossians 3:5. Man in revolt

against God is set adrift. In his subsequent downward slide
from false god to false god he loses track of his own self-
worth, identity, and all sense of moral obligation toward
the world. His neighbor now depends on the variable range
of feelings and interests of man's own confused desire which
determines the dominating motivation for his life since he
is "set free" from obedience to God. His list of sins is intended to stir in the mind of each reader even further words
and experiences that will tell the story of the wholesale
crisis not in theoretical terms but on a human scale.

I believe that we in the twentieth century are able to
understand Paul's analysis. Our own twentieth century "no
god" premises have sold us on the fact that there are no
moral obligations that should merit our anxieties or feelings
of guilt. We have in fact worked very hard to design a social
order without any serious concept of sin—that is personal,
real, unavoidable obligation of the human being before God
and neighbor. And what has been the result for us? Certainly not less hurtfulness between people, not a reduction
in avarice and arrogance between nations. The crisis nevertheless stays on whether or not we acknowledge the threefold moral obligations of Romans chapter 1. But in trying to
avoid accountability our modern western culture has lost
soul power. "The heroine of current fiction has no soul—
she has not even a heart; she has only a nervous system.
She has no spiritual crises: she has only nervous reactions
. . . with the disappearance of the idea of original sin, with
the disappearance of the idea of intense moral struggle, the
human beings presented for us in prose fiction today tend
to become less and less real . . . more and more vaporous"
(T. S. Eliot).

But the escape from sin never finally succeeds. ". . . I
will block up her way with thorns and I will build a wall
against her, so that she cannot find her paths" (Hosea 2:6).

Whether we admit it or not the universe is moral by the
decision of God and sooner or later every person, as well as

his society, must meet up with the thorns we ourselves helped to plant. It is just this kind of basic logic that the Apostle Paul evokes in the opening prosecution section of Romans.

Section 2—Romans 2:1–11

2: 1)Therefore you have no excuse, O man, whoever you are, when you judge another; for in passing judgment upon him you condemn yourself because you, the judge, are doing the very same things. 2)We know that the judgment of God rightly falls upon those who do such things. 3)Do you suppose, O man, that when you judge those who do such things and yet do them yourself, you will escape the judgment of God? 4)Or do you presume upon the riches of his kindness and forbearance and patience? Do you not know that God's kindness is meant to lead you to repentance?

5)But by your hard and impenitent heart you are storing up wrath for yourself on the day of wrath when God's righteous judgment will be revealed. 6)For he will render to every man according to his works: 7)to those who by patience in well-doing seek for glory and honor and immortality, he will give eternal life; 8)but for those who are factious and do not obey the truth, but obey wickedness, there will be wrath and fury. 9) There will be tribulation and distress for every human being who does evil, the Jew first and also the Greek, 10)but glory and honor and peace for every one who does good, the Jew first and also the Greek. 11)For God shows no partiality.

In 2:1–11, Paul makes one further point to establish the case even more completely. He builds a subjective argument and it runs as follows: Whoever of us feels a sense of outrage at the sins of neighbors against our own right to survive, must realize that in the core of that feeling is the admission of the existence of God and of God's law which stands over against all human attempts to build a world outlook that permits the destruction of the neighbor. Therefore, to recognize the guilt, the hurtfulness of others, is to admit to the greater source of truth by which the evaluation was made.

Such an act then brings every man to his own crisis before
God, with or without an actual copy of the decalogue in his
hand. The point is that the law, as Paul treats it in this
passage, is an historical revelation of God's order within the
actual history of Israel, but the subject matter to which the
law bears witness is universally operative whether or not we
are able to recite its chapters and verses. For me "to bear
false witness" against a neighbor, then, goes against the will
of God for my life, and the result is alienation—whether I
happen to know the law's number or the Mosaic wording
is beside the point.

"We can appropriate Paul's judgment which takes Gentiles
and Jews together in their situation before God (Rom.
1:18–3:20) when one understands the universal human significance of the Jewish Law as the explicit formulation of the
universally valid relation between deed and its consequences, as one form of the legal structure of social life
which is realized everywhere in different ways, then the
Jewish people actually represent humanity in general. . . ."[13]

Section 3—Romans 2:12–3:20

> 2: 12)All who have sinned without the law will also
> perish without the law, and all who have sinned under
> the law will be judged by the law. 13)For it is not the
> hearers of the law who are righteous before God, but
> the doers of the law who will be justified. 14)When
> Gentiles who have not the law do by nature what the
> law requires, they are a law to themselves, even though
> they do not have the law. 15)They show that what the
> law requires is written on their hearts, while their
> conscience also bears witness and their conflicting
> thoughts accuse or perhaps excuse them 16)on that
> day when, according to my gospel, God judges the
> secrets of men by Christ Jesus.
> 17)But if you call yourself a Jew and rely upon the
> law and boast of your relation to God 18)and know
> his will and approve what is excellent, because you are
> instructed in the law, 19)and if you are sure that you
> are a guide to the blind, a light to those who are in
> darkness, 20)a corrector of the foolish, a teacher of

children, having in the law the embodiment of knowledge and truth—21)you then who teach others, will
you not teach yourself? While you preach against
stealing, do you steal? 22)You who say that one must
not commit adultery, do you commit adultery? You
who abhor idols, do you rob temples? 23)You who
boast in the law, do you dishonor God by breaking the
law? 24)For, as it is written, "The name of God is
blasphemed among the Gentiles because of you."

25)Circumcision indeed is of value if you obey the
law; but if you break the law, your circumcision becomes uncircumcision. 26)So, if a man who is uncircumcised keeps the precepts of the law, will not his
uncircumcision be regarded as circumcision? 27)Then
those who are physically uncircumcised but keep the
law will condemn you who have the written code and
circumcision but break the law. 28)For he is not a real
Jew who is one outwardly, nor is true circumcision
something external and physical. 29)He is a Jew who
is one inwardly, and real circumcision is a matter of
the heart, spiritual and not literal. His praise is not
from men but from God.

3: 1)Then what advantage has the Jew? Or what is
the value of circumcision? 2)Much in every way. To
begin with, the Jews are entrusted with the oracles of
God. 3)What if some were unfaithful? Does their
faithlessness nullify the faithfulness of God? 4)By no
means! Let God be true though every man be false, as
it is written, "That thou mayest be justified in thy
words, and prevail when thou art judged." 5)But if
our wickedness serves to show the justice of God, what
shall we say? That God is unjust to inflict wrath on
us? (I speak in a human way.) 6)By no means! For
then how could God judge the world? 7)But if through
my falsehood God's truthfulness abounds to his glory,
why am I still being condemned as a sinner? 8)And
why not do evil that good may come?—as some people slanderously charge us with saying. Their condemnation is just.

9) What then? Are we Jews any better off? No, not
at all; for I have already charged that all men, both
Jews and Greeks, are under the power of sin, 10)as
it is written: "None is righteous, no, not one; 11)no one
understands, no one seeks for God. 12)All have turned
aside, together they have gone wrong; no one does
good, not even one." 13)"Their throat is an open
grave, they use their tongues to deceive." "The venom

of asps is under their lips." 14)"Their mouth is full of
curses and bitterness." 15)"Their feet are swift to
shed blood, 16)in their paths are ruin and misery,
17)and the way of peace they do not know." 18)
"There is no fear of God before their eyes." 19)Now
we know that whatever the law says it speaks to those
who are under the law, so that every mouth may be
stopped, and the whole world may be held accountable to God. 20)For no human being will be justified
in his sight by works of the law, since through the
law comes knowledge of sin.

The final part of this section is Paul's elaborate discussion
of the relationship of the Jewish nation to this crisis. Though
historically the Jew is the inheritor of the Law and within
it the identity rite of circumcision, Paul argues that these
benefits—and he insists that they are benefits—are not a
shield for Israel against the claim God makes upon the
chosen people in the Law and in the cultus of Israel. The
real test, then, is not possession of the Law and the tradition
but obedience to what the Law demands and what the cultus
(ceremonial tradition) means. Paul is very pessimistic about
the success of his Jewish contemporaries on the basis of that
all-important criterion: "What then? Are we Jews any better
off? No, not at all; for I have already charged that all men,
both Jews and Greeks, are under the power of sin" (3:9).

Paul not only sketches in the origin of the crisis, he also
teaches the cumulative nature of the crisis. "Nothing stays
put for us," says Blaise Pascal in *Pensées*.

As we have noted in 1:18–23, the idolatries deteriorate.
They spiral downward from "images resembling man" to
"images resembling reptiles."

Also, the list of sins in 1:28–32 are by nature cumulative,
which is noted by both the intensity of word choice and
the final comment that the Apostle chooses to make in verse
32, "though they know God's decree . . . they not only do
them but approve those who practice them." Here is the
most intense form of moral obliquity, and the Apostle means

to etch in the horror of this downward spiral by the use of the positive verb *approve* in the context of four negatives: "foolish, faithless, heartless, ruthless" (1:31). Paul leaves it to the Romans to find their own social and personal illustrations of his analysis. There it stands—not only that concrete, interpersonal sins result from a broken relationship with God, but that the sins of today do not remain static—a fixed point that we will be able to locate tomorrow. There is a dynamic forcefulness within the sins themselves; hurtfulness is a moving point, a cumulative reality that spirals beyond anything anticipated at the beginning.

The reader's own involvement in the crisis also intensifies and cumulates in Paul's prosecution section. The text begins impersonally and in general terms: ". . . wickedness of men who by *their* wickedness . . . so *they* are without excuse" (1:18). In 2:1, Paul tightens the circle with the more direct second person, "Therefore, *you* have no excuse, O man, whoever you are." In 2:17, the circle is tightened still smaller as the Apostle considers the Jewish reader: "Are *we* Jews any better off?" Finally, in one passage Paul even exclaims: ". . . Why am *I* still being condemned as a sinner? . . . Their condemnation is just" (3:7).

The whole force of the passage is to show dramatically the cumulative nature of the crisis in degrees of intensity; not only the deterioration of idols or of sin, but also of obligation, guilt. ". . . so that every mouth may be stopped, and the whole world may be held accountable to God . . ." (3:19).

In a stunning single passage (3:10–18), Paul brings together a group of Old Testament quotations primarily from the Psalms to proof-text his contention that Jews and Greeks universally share in the same problem.

The origin of the human crisis is the broken relationship between mankind and God. This crisis quickly spreads not only within the self but outwardly toward the whole creation. What then shall be the solution for such a wholescale problem? Is it the Law of God? Paul's answer is no. His reasoning: the Law is not adequate to resolve the crisis because of its own inherent limitations. "For no human being will be justified in (God's) sight by works of the law, since through the law comes knowledge of sin" (3:20). What the Law succeeds in doing it does well; namely, in compounding guilt, of rightly portraying the extent of man's brokenness; but the implication is that the need of mankind is more complex. Nothing short of "total help for total need" (Karl Barth). The law is static, but the crisis is spiraling, in continuous movement. Therefore, there must be the help that is strong and dynamic enough within itself that it is able to overtake and outdistance a cumulating crisis.

Part 4

Cumulative Grace

Section 1—Romans 3:21–31

> 3: 21)But now the righteousness of God has been manifested apart from law, although the law and the prophets bear witness to it, 22)the righteousness of God through faith in Jesus Christ for all who believe. For there is no distinction; 23)since all have sinned and fall short of the glory of God, 24)they are justified by his grace as a gift, through the redemption which is in Christ Jesus, 25)whom God put forward as an expiation by his blood, to be received by faith. This was to show God's righteousness, because in his divine forbearance he had passed over former sins; 26)it was to prove at the present time that he himself is righteous and that he justifies him who has faith in Jesus.
>
> 27)Then what becomes of our boasting? It is excluded. On what principle? On the principle of works? No, but on the principle of faith. 28)For we hold that a man is justified by faith apart from works of law. 29)Or is God the God of Jews only? Is he not the God of Gentiles also? Yes, of Gentiles also, 30)since God is one; and he will justify the circumcised on the ground of their faith and the uncircumcised through their faith. 31)Do we then overthrow the law by this faith? By no means! On the contrary, we uphold the law.

"But now the righteousness of God." Paul, the attorney for the prosecution, crosses the courtroom stage to speak for the defense. It soon becomes clear that one greater than Paul is in fact not only the true prosecutor but also the redeemer of humanity. Three themes emerge within the first few sentences of this great defense: (1) The total adequacy and completeness of God's redemption of man is affirmed. (2) That because of the greatness of this redemption there occurs on the side of grace a leveling of humanity as whole-scale and total as was the case on the side of judgment (1:18–3:20). (3) Therefore the immensity of God's redemptive act requires of men and women only faith; to add one further ingredient ignores the fact of the leveling and diminishes the gift of God.

1. "But now God has spoken for himself apart from the law though the law and prophets bear witness to his speech" (3:21).

Paul's opening statement establishes his thesis. God's act, his own self-revealing word and work in Jesus Christ is not so much a part or further extension of the Old Testament Law, so in that instance Christ would then be definable from within the expectations of the Law. Rather it is the reverse. The central fact of all history is the event Jesus Christ, and it is the Law and prophets which receive their meaning and purpose from him. The fact is that the Law and the prophets gain their own true meaning in that they attest to the primacy of Jesus Christ.

The result of God's act is redemption "for *all* who believe. For there is no distinction."

It now becomes Paul's purpose to begin his teaching concerning the meaning of that redemption. The reader of Romans is first of all impressed by the words and images that Paul here makes use of to express the act of God for the world. "Paul has thus pressed into service the language of the law court (justified), the slave market (redemption), and the temple (expiation) to do justice to the fullness of God's gracious act in Christ; pardon, liberation, atonement.

. . ."[1] As the Book of Romans continues to unfold, the vocabulary will keep on growing: "salvation," first used in chapter 1:16 will appear again (5:9, 10:10); "reconciliation" (5:10); "acquittal" (5:18); "life" (5:18, 6:23); "election" (8:33, 9:11, 11:28); "wild olive shoot grafted in" (11:17); "welcomed" (15:7). These words together with "grace," "mercy," "peace," "love," are all used to describe the redemption won for man by the death and resurrection of Christ. This richness of the salvation vocabulary within the Book of Romans by its very complexity points up the wholescale nature of the redemption event.

What do the words mean? Put another way, how does Paul explain the meaning for mankind of Christ's death? What is his theology of redemption? "At the right time Christ died for the ungodly . . ." (5:6). Redemption doctrine in Romans develops along three main lines.

(A) The first interpretive concept that Paul speaks of is found in the word translated "expiation" (rsv) or "propitiation" (av): "Whom God put forward as an expiation by his blood" (3:25). In secular Greek the word meant "to placate," and in the sense of men seeking to justify themselves before the gods. In the Septuagint "expiation" is used to refer to the Hebrew word "mercy seat" of the Ark within the holiest of holies for the Day of Atonement sacrifice—literally the *covering*, the symbolic resolution of sins by the sprinkling of the blood of sacrifice. Paul is therefore teaching us that "the death of Christ is the means by which God does away with the people's sin—not symbolically, as in the ritual of Leviticus 16, but actually and historically, once and for all."[2] The Old Testament expectation is now completed and made actual by the sacrifice of Jesus Christ—not of a ram caught in the thicket (Gen. 22:13), not by the priestly sacrifices in the Temple, but by the event on Good Friday. What then has happened? God himself has made the sacrifice once and for all. The completed verb tenses confirm this sense of finality. God himself becomes the representative,

the substitute for man, the expiation, and so grants to us all
the liberation from sin as a gift to be received by faith.

(B) Another theological understanding of salvation is introduced in 4:24 following Paul's lengthy discussion of
Abraham's faith. He maintains that the righteousness reckoned to Abraham because of his faith will be reckoned also
to us, whether we are Jews or not, when we also have faith.
"It will be reckoned to us who believe in him that raised from
the dead Jesus our Lord, *who was put to death for our trespasses and raised for our justification*" (4:24, 25). In this
sentence Paul teaches that the death of Jesus is only fully
understood when it is seen together with his resurrection.
On Good Friday *and* Easter the victory has been won which
brings justification. Luther asks in his Catechism: "What
hath Christ won for us by his death and resurrection?"
Answer: "He has won the battle against the power of the
Devil, against sin and against death" (Martin Luther). Paul
teaches in 4:24, 25, that the victory is now disclosed by
the actual triumph of Jesus Christ over death. The result of
the victory is "reckoned righteousness" for those who believe.
It is "alien righteousness," that is, outside ourselves, granted
to mankind by God's act.

(C) The Apostle has even more to say: If it is true that
the cross is the perfect sacrifice, if the cross because of Easter
is the victory over sin, death and Satan, what other theme is
present? There is another thread present in Paul's portrayal:
The cross is the revelation of the love of God. "Justified by
God's grace as a gift, through the redemption that is in
Christ Jesus" (3:24). In Romans 5 Paul makes a further
comment upon this third thread: "God shows his love for us
in that while we were yet sinners Christ died for us" (5:8).
Paul is plainly teaching in these two quotations (3:24 and
5:8) that if I am to ask, "What happened at the cross?" I
will answer, "At the cross I discovered that the love of God
is for *me*." Paul reminds the Romans of this third thread

in 8:31–32: ". . . God is for us. . . . He who did not spare his own son but gave him up for us all. . . ." Because of the event of the mighty love of God "he who has faith in Jesus is justified" (3:26).

These three understandings of the cross of Christ are not independent doctrinally from each other but are threads of the same great cord. In order to develop a whole understanding of redemption theology two kinds of questions must be asked, the first is primarily *objective* and the second is primarily *subjective*. The first question is this: "What has God done?" (an objective–subjective question); and secondly "What has happened to man because of what God has done?" (a subjective–objective question).

The objective fact of the gospel as Paul teaches in 3:21–5:21 is that what God has done at Good Friday and Easter is his own sovereign act. Whether we men appreciate or experience or understand God's love and sacrifice and victory is secondary. The *fact* is that God has manifested his grace. In spite of man's sin God's love stands (5:6–8). The event of the cross is just that—an event; it is historically *extra nos* (outside ourselves). The cross event however is also a personal event—God's very inner nature is revealed to us. "Christ *died* for the ungodly." Because the cross is the *personal* event of God the salvation message in the New Testament never becomes theoretical soteriology, objective truth catalogued and applied by teachers of religion, "salvation by mimeograph." But on the other hand because the cross is an *event* the salvation message in the New Testament is not subjective to where the theological meaning of the cross is only as meaningful as our feelings are able to comprehend. In my view the current situation in Protestant theology is dangerously imperiled by an *ad nos* (toward ourselves) existentialism by which we have tended to create models of relevancy on the basis of our own expectations and felt needs. In this way redemption is not first of all objective but existential. The result is that the kerygma of the New Testament is subjected and brought under our own control.

> Since the days of Schleiermacher, Protestant theology has shown a tendency to interpret the divine attributes in terms of personal experience. Such a view entailed a twofold weakening of the biblical message. God was thereby reduced to the rank of a psychic factor. He was considered the subject of man's religious priori.[3]

But Paul insists upon the objective reality of Good Friday and Easter, quite independent of our felt needs or priorities; the fact stands independently of our categories: "Christ died for the ungodly."

But now it may be asked, What is the subjective impact of the cross? What has happened to and within men and women because of what God has done? The answer to this question is a major theme of Romans, and Paul will address the questions in many different ways. The key words of 3:21–26 set the stage for the remainder of the book. The key words are: "justified"—to set right (3:24); "redemption"—to set free (3:24); "expiation"—to take the place of (3:25).

Because of Christ's act, we are no longer guilty of sin; we are free in Christ; we are now identified with Christ who took our place at the cross.

2. A second theme is also present in 3:21–31. It is a secondary point for Paul, but nevertheless receives extensive discussion for pastoral as well as theological reasons. That theme is introduced by these words, "The righteousness of God through faith in Jesus Christ for *all* who believe. *For there is no distinction*" (3:22).

No distinction! Paul teaches a fourth result of the cross. As all men and women were made level one toward the other in the crisis of sin (1:18–3:20)—"there is none righteous, no not one . . ." (3:10)—so, in an even more wondrous sense, all men and women are made level one toward the other because of the cross and victory of Jesus Christ. Family or tribal heritage is radically reinterpreted by Paul. Since the fulfillment of every Old Testament tribal longing is now in Christ made complete, what matters and only what matters now is the relationship with Christ. "He will justify the Jew on the ground of their faith and the non-Jew through their faith" (3:30).

3. Martin Luther translated Romans 3:28 as follows, "For we hold that a man is justified by faith *only* apart from works of law." Joachim Jeremias[4] comments that linguistically Luther is correct in his addition of *only* in his German text of Romans because that addition helps to capture the contextual force of Paul's total argument in 3:21–31. Paul argues throughout chapter 4 that neither works of the law (4:13) nor tribal heritage (4:16–25) may add any requirement or obligation beyond the requirement that God himself makes—and that is faith alone. "That is why it depends on faith, in order that the promise may rest on grace . . ." (4:16).

What does Paul mean by the word faith? Within these verses of chapters 3, 4, and 5 faith is introduced to us. The far-reaching implications of faith will surface throughout the letter as an enlargement of what is simply stated in these early sentences.

The Greek word for faith (as with the words for grace, love, prayer, and others) receives its meaning in the New Testament by its usage. Let me cite one textual example from Romans to show how the word faith is defined by the Apostle.

In 4:20 he tells us of Abraham, "No distrust made him waver concerning the promise of God, he was fully convinced that God was able to do what he had promised." In this text faith is portrayed as Abraham's wager upon the

trustworthiness of God. Faith in Romans as throughout
the Bible is always the response of people (the person) to
the character of the Lord himself. "Whom God put forward
. . . to be received by faith" (3:25). Faith is the profoundly
personal trust in the speech of God himself.

He is the line between Almighty God and man set free
from any exchange, opened on our side toward the God who
made us and seeks us out.

Section 2—Romans 4:1–25—ABRAHAM

4: 1)What then shall we say about Abraham, our
forefather according to the flesh? 2)For if Abraham
was justified by works, he has something to boast
about, but not before God. 3)For what does the scripture say? "Abraham believed God, and it was reckoned
to him as righteousness." 4)Now to one who works, his
wages are not reckoned as a gift but as his due. 5)And
to one who does not work but trusts him who justifies
the ungodly, his faith is reckoned as righteousness. 6)
So also David pronounces a blessing upon the man to
whom God reckons righteousness apart from works:
7)"Blessed are those whose iniquities are forgiven,
and whose sins are covered; 8)blessed is the man
against whom the Lord will not reckon his sin." 9)Is
this blessing pronounced only upon the circumcised,
or also upon the uncircumcised? We say that faith was
reckoned to Abraham as righteousness, 10)How then
was it reckoned to him? Was it before or after he had
been circumcised? It was not after, but before he was
circumcised. 11)He received circumcision as a sign or

seal of the righteousness which he had by faith while he was still uncircumcised.

The purpose was to make him the father of all who believe without being circumcised and who thus have righteousness reckoned to them, 12)and likewise the father of the circumcised who are not merely circumcised but also follow the example of the faith which our father Abraham had before he was circumcised. 13)The promise to Abraham and his descendants, that they should inherit the world, did not come through the law but through the righteousness of faith. 14)If it is the adherents of the law who are to be the heirs, faith is null and the promise is void.

15)For the law brings wrath, but where there is no law there is no transgression. 16)That is why it depends on faith, in order that the promise may rest on grace and be guaranteed to all his descendants—not only to the adherents of the law but also to those who share the faith of Abraham, for he is the father of us all, 17)as it is written, "I have made you the father of many nations"—in the presence of the God in whom he believed, who gives life to the dead and calls into existence the things that do not exist. 18)In hope he believed against hope, that he should become the father of many nations; as he had been told, "So shall your descendants be."

19)He did not weaken in faith when he considered his own body, which was as good as dead because he was about a hundred years old, or when he considered the barrenness of Sarah's womb. 20)No distrust made him waver concerning the promise of God, but he grew strong in his faith as he gave glory to God, 21) fully convinced that God was able to do what he had promised. 22)That is why his faith was "reckoned to him as righteousness." 23)But the words, "it was reckoned to him," were written not for his sake alone, 24) but for ours also. It will be reckoned to us who believe in him that raised from the dead Jesus our Lord, 25)who was put to death for our trespasses and raised for our justification.

"Abraham believed God." Within chapter 4 Paul interprets the significance of Abraham and David in the context of grace and faith. Paul concludes that the identity rite of circumcision, which had been a major issue for Paul and

members of the church of Galatia (see Gal. 2:1–10), is
rightly understood as a sign that followed Abraham's faith.
That is, according to Paul, the ritual of circumcision was
secondary to the faith even for Abraham. Therefore, Paul
argues, those who have faith and who are not "merely
circumcised" are the real children of Abraham, since they
follow the experience that was Abraham's.

Not content simply to make the matter clear concerning
rituals, he goes on to teach the primacy of faith over the
Law itself in 4:13–15. The promise to Abraham (Gen. 12:1–
3) actually precedes the Law by four hundred years (Gal.
3:17) and is not in any way replaced by the Law of Moses.

Paul reflects upon the faith of Abraham concerning God's
promise, "I have made you the father of many nations."
Paul unites Abraham, father of Israel, to Abraham father of
all who have faith in God—"father of many nations." He
shows that the promise to Abraham is truly fulfilled in the
belief of the first-century Gentiles in Jesus Christ.

Paul's interpretation of Abraham maintains that at the
very origins of Israel, and within the Abrahamic covenant
itself, the plan of God is promised to include all nations
within the covenant. For Paul, the universal relevance of
God's intention is clear at the origins of the tribe of Abraham.
Therefore, Israel of all people cannot depend upon or boast
of exclusive rites such as circumcision. God's decision stands
at the beginnings of Abraham's people, and that decision,
Paul reminds his readers, includes all who have faith.

On the basis of this chapter, the sphere of the holy promise and plan of God stretches far beyond narrowly conceived
boundaries of Jewish nationalism.

Section 3—Romans 5:1–21—THE TWO ADAMS

> 5:1) Therefore, since we are justified by faith, we have
> peace with God through our Lord Jesus Christ. 2)
> Through him we have obtained access to this grace in
> which we stand, and we rejoice in our hope of sharing
> the glory of God. 3)More than that, we rejoice in our

sufferings, knowing that suffering produces endurance, 4)and endurance produces character, and character produces hope, 5)and hope does not disappoint us, because God's love has been poured into our hearts through the Holy Spirit which has been given to us. 6)While we were yet helpless, at the right time Christ died for the ungodly. 7)Why, one will hardly die for a righteous man—though perhaps for a good man one will dare even to die. 8)But God shows his love for us in that while we were yet sinners Christ died for us.

9)Since, therefore, we are now justified by his blood, much more shall we be saved by him from the wrath of God. 10)For if while we were enemies we were reconciled to God by the death of his Son, much more, now that we are reconciled, shall we be saved by his life. 11)Not only so, but we also rejoice in God through our Lord Jesus Christ, through whom we have now received our reconciliation.

12)Therefore as sin came into the world through one man and death through sin, and so death spread to all men because all men sinned— 13)sin indeed was in the world before the law was given, but sin is not counted where there is no law. 14)Yet death reigned from Adam to Moses, even over those whose sins were not like the transgression of Adam, who was a type of the one who was to come. 15)But the free gift is not like the trespass. For if many died through one man's trespass, much more have the grace of God and the free gift in the grace of that one man Jesus Christ abounded for many. 16)And the free gift is not like the effect of that one man's sin. For the judgment following one trespass brought condemnation, but the free gift following many trespasses brings justification. 17)If, because of one man's trespass, death reigned through that one man, much more will those who receive the abundance of grace and the free gift of righteousness reign in life through the one man Jesus Christ.

18)Then as one man's trespass led to condemnation for all men, so one man's act of righteousness leads to acquittal and life for all men. 19)For as by one man's disobedience many were made sinners, so by one man's obedience many will be made righteous. 20)Law came in, to increase the trespass; but where sin increased, grace abounded all the more, 21)so that, as sin reigned in death, grace also might reign through righteousness to eternal life through Jesus Christ our Lord.

In my view 5:1 begins with a summary as the Apostle
regathers his argument from chapter 1:18 forward.

"While we were yet helpless. . . ." With these words,
Paul develops a model to explain what he has written so
far. A diagram may be useful in portraying this summary:

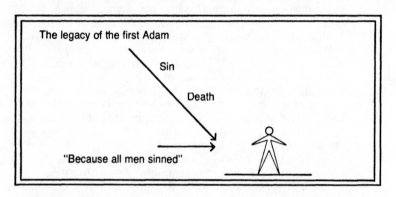

In the first half of the model, Paul teaches that all men
(represented by one figure) share universally in the same
legacy of the first man, Adam. Paul, however, preserves
human freedom in the phrase "because all men sinned." His
theological argument then in 5:12–14 is as follows: Every
human being shares with every other human being in the
same crisis, that is, the crisis of sin and death. The Law of
Moses does not alter the basic situation, even though the
presence of the Law intensifies the crisis by providing a
means of measurement, a plumb line held over against the
people and our proud towers.

But the crisis is universal in that, whether classified or
measured, the sins of men work their damage, so that in this
fact all humanity is seen in equal terms. This teaching of
Paul is referred to theologically as the doctrine of original
sin. What is a surprise to us is to discover that for Paul the
doctrine of original sin is a doctrine in behalf of man not
against him! It forms one important element in the biblical
teaching on the inescapable solidarity of all persons; it

sweeps away every pretense of the superiority of one person over against another. Think of the doctrine in these terms. It is like three ship passengers who happen to get washed overboard in mid-Atlantic. The reasons for slipping off the deck vary from individual to individual (verse 14). Each individual retains his distinctiveness in the water as on the deck (verse 12). But as each one discovers his own plight and finds his companions also in the same cold water, it is meaningless to discuss or debate degrees of fault, status of privileges (one is first class, the other economy), individual swimming skill (those with skill in the Law and tradition vs. those without). The point is that the realization of the immensity of the crisis has established new priorities and has created a new solidarity in that each of the three now knows the meaning of *total* need "for which the *only* hope is *total* help."[5]

Advice on the latest long distance swimming techniques is valueless precisely because of the wholesale nature of this solidarity of every man with the first Adam. We are all in this together; we share a cumulative crisis together.

This is Paul's argument.

(This mixture of individual and total need is also forcefully portrayed in the Old Testament theophany of Isaiah 6. "Woe is *me* . . . in the midst of a sinful people.")

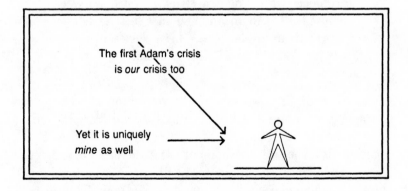

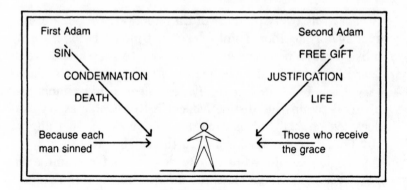

But now in 5:15–21 the Apostle completes the model with his affirmation of the second Adam—the one who brings to man a new and better legacy—the legacy of grace: Jesus Christ is that man.

Paul teaches that mankind is not only the recipient of the legacy of the first Adam but he is also the recipient of the legacy of the second Adam. As in the first legacy, Paul dialectically preserves the freedom of the "every man," so in the legacy of grace the freedom of faith is also preserved. "Those who receive . . ." (verse 17).

The most far-reaching theological discussion of this crucial chapter 5 is found in Karl Barth's *Commentary*. He has this comment:

> The two factors are not of equal weight and importance; nor is there a strict balance between them. Life in Adam and life in Christ is not an ever-recurring cycle. . . . Christ does not merely expose a distinction. He forces a *decision* between the two factors. . . .[6]

As the crisis is wholesale so the resolution is wholesale; nothing need be added to it except that we trust the gift. But by no means is that act of trusting a small matter. Karl Barth calls it the "critical moment." It is the crisis of greatest significance because, as Paul will affirm in chapter 12, it means the final exposure of all of our other gods. The thirty-eight-pound statue of Diana is no help for the three swimmers in mid-Atlantic. Adore her as they once did she is now only excess weight in the water. False gods cannot resolve the deepest crisis.

T. S. Eliot in *Journey of the Magi* saw the issue of the critical moment, and puts it powerfully into the speech of one of the wise men who reflects upon his journey to see the Christ Child at Bethlehem. "Was that a birth?" "No— I have seen birth, that was no birth—it was death—death to all our gods. . . ."

Finally, Paul once again integrates the Old Testament Law into this overview. It is portrayed as if it were a measuring line which in the last analysis reveals to us the full dimensions of the problem. It is Paul's conclusion that such knowledge of the Law has only the value of intensifying the dilemma. The swimmer with the Law is the one who had been watching the maps closely and therefore is the one who rightly informs his companions of their true distance from New York and Southampton. In this regard the treatment of the Law in Romans 3, 4, and 5, is a further commentary by Paul upon his decisive statement concerning the Law in Galatians 3:23–25.

> Now before faith came, we were confined under the law, kept under restraint until faith should be revealed. So that the law was our schoolmaster until Christ came, that we might be justified by faith. But now that faith has come we are no longer under a schoolmaster. . . .

The Law is a friend of ours, as it is meant to bring us to the only source of help able to heal the illnesses diagnosed and even compounded by the revelations of the Law, but which of itself never was, is, or will be able to provide the cure. We need a solution able to heal broken relationships and to outdistance a cumulative crisis.

But where sin cumulates, the grace of God is able to over-

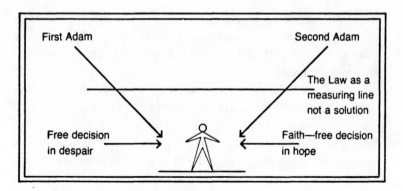

take and outdistance even the most devastating and cumulative tragedy of man.

Just as there is established in the legacy of the first Adam a solidarity among men, so, that real solidarity is even more profoundly sealed in the legacy of the second Adam. The Christian is one who receives the gift of life in Jesus Christ, or to use Paul's word in his prologue to the book, the one who *obeys* Jesus Christ, the Lord. ". . . Jesus Christ our Lord, through whom we have received grace and apostleship to bring about the obedience of faith. . . ." (1:5).

There is one further question that Romans 5 poses for the reader: How do I as a Christian understand my neighbor in the perspective of the two legacies of Romans 5? Whether the neighbor is a believer or not, I have discovered in the gospel the prior fact of both his *need* and *belovedness* and I see him in the context of that whole reality. Jesus Christ has already loved the world; he has already died in the world's behalf; therefore, the ground of human worth is settled before we were even born. My neighbor does not become meaningful either to God or to me only after he believes, but his ground of meaning is rooted in God's decision. The decision was made before he trusts in that good decision, or is personally aware of it to the degree that he believes its good news. The ethical impact of both legacies upon the Christian's relationship with the world is as wholescale as is the event that makes it a reality.

Part 5

Being a Christian

A Preface

Paul, who was the prosecutor (1:18–3:20) and the defense attorney (3:21–5:21) in the opening of Romans, now assumes a stance which is more pastoral and personal. Paul's personal feelings and his own spiritual pilgrimage become major ingredients in chapters 6–8, in contrast to the more objective theological outlook of the earlier chapters of the book. Paul continues to be a teacher as before, but the intensity of his own involvement is heightened. The clue to this part of Romans is found in the opening sentence, "What shall we say then?" These five words do more than simply introduce the first question of this third great argument of Romans; they also form the title of the whole. *If what has been affirmed regarding the wholesale intervention of Almighty God in our behalf is really true then what difference does it all make in our daily lives?* In this remarkable section the apostle will share with us his Christian journey and his own discovery of the meaning of the Christian life. In chapter 6 he will set forth the strong claim placed upon the Christian together with the grace that underpins that claim. In chapter 7 he will tell in realistic and personal terms of the contest that the Christian is engaged in as the doctrine

67

of sanctification is clarified. Then in chapter 8 he will review the general thesis and develop the theology of the Holy Spirit.

Consider these three main lines of thought as they emerge in the text.

Section 1—Romans 6:1-7:13—THE THIRD CROSSROAD

6: 1)What shall we say then? Are we to continue in sin that grace may abound? 2)By no means! How can we who died to sin still live in it? 3)Do you not know that all of us who have been baptized into Christ Jesus were baptized into his death? 4)We were buried therefore with him by baptism into death, so that as Christ was raised from the dead by the glory of the Father, we too might walk in newness of life. 5)For if we have been united with him in a death like his, we shall certainly be united with him in a resurrection like his.

6)We know that our old self was crucified with him so that the sinful body might be destroyed, and we might no longer be enslaved to sin. 7)For he who has died is freed from sin. 8)But if we have died with Christ, we believe that we shall also live with him. 9) For we know that Christ being raised from the dead will never die again; death no longer has dominion over him. 10)The death he died he died to sin, once for all, but the life he lives he lives to God. 11)So you also must consider yourselves dead to sin and alive to God in Christ Jesus. 12)Let not sin therefore reign in your mortal bodies, to make you obey their passions.

13)Do not yield your members to sin as instruments of wickedness, but yield yourselves to God as men who have been brought from death to life, and your members to God as instruments of righteousness. 14) For sin will have no dominion over you, since you are not under law but under grace. 15)What then? Are we to sin because we are not under law but under grace? By no means! 16)Do you not know that if you yield yourselves to any one as obedient slaves, you are slaves of the one whom you obey, either of sin, which leads to death, or of obedience, which leads to righteousness? 17)But thanks be to God, that you who were once slaves of sin have become obedient from the heart to the standard of teaching to which you were committed, 18)and, having been set free from sin, have become slaves of righteousness.

19)I am speaking in human terms, because of your natural limitations. For just as you once yielded your members to impurity and to greater and greater iniquity, so now yield your members to righteousness for sanctification. 20)When you were slaves of sin, you were free in regard to righteousness. 21)But then what return did you get from the things of which you are now ashamed? The end of those things is death. 22) But now that you have been set free from sin and have become slaves of God, the return you get is sanctification and its end, eternal life. 23)For the wages of sin is death, but the free gift of God is eternal life in Christ Jesus our Lord.

7: 1)Do you not know, brethren—for I am speaking to those who know the law—that the law is binding on a person only during his life? 2)Thus a married woman is bound by law to her husband as long as he lives; but if her husband dies she is discharged from the law concerning the husband. 3)Accordingly, she will be called an adulteress if she lives with another man while her husband is alive. But if her husband dies she is free from that law, and if she marries another man she is not an adulteress. 4)Likewise, my brethren, you have died to the law through the body of Christ, so that you may belong to another, to him who has been raised from the dead in order that we may bear fruit for God. 5)While we were living in the flesh, our sinful passions, aroused by the law, were at work in our members to bear fruit for death. 6)But now we are discharged from the law, dead to that which held us captive, so that we serve not under the old written code but in the new life of the Spirit.

7)What then shall we say? That the law is sin? By no means! Yet, if it had not been for the law, I should not have known sin. I should not have known what it is to covet if the law had not said, "You shall not covet." 8)But sin, finding opportunity in the commandment, wrought in me all kinds of covetousness. Apart from the law sin lies dead. 9)I was once alive apart from the law, but when the commandment came, sin revived and I died; 10)the very commandment which promised life proved to be death to me. 11)For sin, finding opportunity in the commandment, deceived me and by it killed me. 12)So the law is holy, and the commandment is holy and just and good.

13)Did that which is good, then, bring death to me?
By no means! It was sin, working death in me through
what is good, in order that sin might be shown to be
sin, and through the commandment might become
sinful beyond measure.

"What shall we say then? Are we to continue in sin that
grace may abound? By no means! How can we who died to
sin still live in it?" (6:1–2).

Paul makes it clear at the outset that he has no intention
of producing a crowd of escape artists who welcome the love
of God as a gift or an energy but not as a way of life. God's
grace is not an "elemental Spirit" (see Col. 2:20), or a divine
benefit to be incorporated into the collection of various religious or spiritual values that first-century man might have
desired to turn on and off at will. Paul has compelled his
readers by means of the question in 6:1 to face up to the
third critical crossroads of the Book of Romans.

(1) 1:18–3:20 confronted us with the total nature of the
human crisis, the first crossroad.

(2) 3:21–5:21 confronted us with the total nature of the
answer of God to that crisis, the second crossroad.

(3) 6:1–8:39 now confronts us with the total nature of the
response that we men and women must make in our
answer to God's speech, the third crossroad.

At this point we must try to understand the psychological
and sociological setting into which Paul's challenging question is posed. Paul's question and subsequent discussion reveals how wise and subtle his understanding is of the
ideological mood of his own century.

He is aware that there are some, perhaps many, of his own
generation who are eager to welcome everything taught by
the prosecutor Paul in the hard judgment passages of 1:18–
3:20. These are people conditioned psychologically and
philosophically to accept the worst news possible about
every human situation and relationship. By the first century,
the Greek philosophical climate had experienced some

fatigue after 400 years of ideological dominance. This re-
sulted in a pervasive kind of cynicism on every side. The
blatant decadence of the first-century Mediterranean world
reinforced this cynical outlook to such a point that a whole
circle of thinking people has concluded that there can be
no hope within the historical situation, but only in some form
of escape out of the real world. One escape is death, which
in the Greek view means the setting free of the immortal
soul from the body prison; a second hope would be escape
from the crisis by means of spiritual powers which would
then enable the elevation of knowledge, wisdom, and spirit
over against body, flesh, and earth. But in both views the
prospects are bleak for man to be seen as a whole being—
here and now, alive in the real world. The stoic prayer of
Cleanthes' *Hymn to Zeus* dramatically points out the extent
of this cynicism. ". . . Therefore all-giving Zeus, clouded
in darkness . . . save men from their miserable foolishness,
banish them, O father, from their souls and let them acquire
reason. . . ."

The point is that Paul's prosecution in 1:18–3:20 seems to
confirm the pessimistic appraisal of first-century Stoics,
Platonists, Aristotelians, and even the more easygoing
Epicureans. There have been so many disappointments! Paul
the angry young man of 1:18–3:20 has apparently joined
their ranks.

But the breakthrough of 3:21–5:21, *cumulative grace for
cumulative crises,* surprises the deserts of pessimistic despair
like a monsoon and startles the reader of Romans with a new
radical immensity, the immensity of the act of God in behalf
of the whole world.

There is a question that arises at this point as well: How
will the first-century person, who was willing to accept the
prior outlines of 1:18–3:20, now react to the breakthrough of
3:21–5:21 in Paul's Gospel of God? Does the first-century
person proceed to incorporate this fact of cumulative grace
into the *Hymn to Zeus;* in other words, does he take hold of

the cumulative grace of Romans 5 and define it in the terms
of his own expectation of what salvation would be like for
him—namely escape from the real world into the platonic
world of true idea? In this case, Jesus Christ becomes the
psychic factor, the spiritual secret, the special knowledge
(*gnosis*), the redeemer force, which along with the rest of
the Greek gods would aid a first-century Jonathan Livingston Seagull to transcend his mere seagullness (specific
weight and specific wing span) into the more exciting spirit
realm of unlimited idea.

As I understand Paul's purpose in chapters 6, 7, and 8,
his primary goal is to preserve the essential integrity of the
gift of God's amazing grace from the captivity of Greek
philosophic expectation in the same way that chapters 2, 3,
and 4 had sought to preserve the gospel from the captivity of
the nationalistic–legalistic expectations of his own Jewish
heritage.

Put another way, my contention is that the question of
6:1 and Paul's teaching in 6, 7, and 8 is not only concerned
with the persistent problem of the law and legalism, but also,
and of even greater importance, these chapters reveal Paul's
concern for what can correctly be described as the Pre-
Gnostic attack upon the integrity of the gospel. This attack
was beginning to surface at the time of the writing of the
New Testament, and would by the close of the first century
be a fully developed movement. One of the results of the
discovery of the Gnostic Library in Nag Nammadi, Egypt,
1945, is that we now realize that the Gnostic movements had
an earlier start than scholars had previously been able to
accept.

Let me explain the use of the term *Gnostic*. Gnosticism/
Proto-Gnosticism/Pre-Gnosticism refer to the attempt to incorporate the message about Christ, once it is adapted and
sufficiently spiritualized, into a previously established framework so that the Gnostics' own original premises concerning
the nature of reality, the nature of man, the nature of hope,

are preserved while at the same moment "Christ" is included in that framework. The "Christ" of this movement is, as a result, no longer the Jesus Christ of the cross and empty tomb but instead a source of spiritual energy that aids in the escape by man's spiritual self from the world.

Rudolph Bultmann[1] and his school of New Testament interpreters have proposed a theory that contends for the existence of a fully formed gnostic redeemer thesis *prior* to the writing of the New Testament documents. In his view it is the New Testament writers and preachers who are at work molding their gospel about Jesus out of the redemption myths of the Greeks already fully formed and complete. Therefore, if his contention were to prevail the New Testament Gospel owes its redemption themes to the Greek philosophical source as well as, and perhaps in an even greater degree than, to the life and ministry of Jesus. It is his conclusion that the New Testament documents, Matthew, Mark, Luke, and in particular, John, all bear the identifiable influences of the pre-Christian Gnostic premises. For example, James Robinson[2] particularly notes the Gnostic preference for "ascetic private religiosity, the unworldly Apocalyptic." He then maintains that wherever these themes, he calls them "trajectories," are noted in the New Testament documents, the properly trained critic is able to assign to them their correct Gnostic source.

The scholarly foundation for the Bultmannian thesis has rested upon Professor Reitzenstein's work upon third- and fourth-century Gnostic Manichaean and Mandaean texts. During the past few years this crucial assumption of Professor Bultmann has been under reevaluation, and there is now developing a piece-by-piece disintegration of Bultmann's position. It was assumed by Bultmann that these Manichaean and Mandaean Gnostic materials were indicators of very old and in fact pre-Christian Gnostic schools.

But the fact is, we have no actual evidence of these fully formed Gnostic redemption convictions, but rather what we do have is evidence of an outlook by the intellectuals of the Greek world which can rightly be called Pre-Gnostic or Incipient Gnosticism. This is quite a different matter than the thesis of Bultmann. It is the difference between on the one side a Gnostic system which becomes the foundation from which the early church builds its doctrines about Jesus; or on the other side, the existence of an incipient Gnostic frame of reference which upon encountering the New Testament church's proclamation of Jesus Christ seeks then to capture the Jesus of the gospel, and draw him into its own philosophical framework. The evidence of first-century research has pointed overwhelmingly to the second option.

The most recent commentary on John's Gospel by Dr. Raymond E. Brown of Union Seminary, New York, which is presently the most definitive study of the fourth Gospel, is a case in point. Dr. Brown concludes: "The oldest forms of Mandaean theology known to us are to be dated relatively late in the Christian era, and there is no possibility that John was influenced by this thought as we now know it. . . ."[3] Dr. H. J. W. Drijvers writes: "Nowhere do we find a pure form of gnosticism, always it is built upon earlier pre-existing religions or on their traditions."

The most telling explanation has come in the book by Professor Edwin Yamauchi.[4] "The Gnostic Redeemer figure as described by Reitzenstein and Bultmann, and as attested in the Manichaean and Mandaean texts, is simply a post-Christian development dependent upon the figure of Christ, rather than a pre-Christian myth upon which the New Testament figure of Christ depends.

"We have indications of an attitude, an outlook . . . 'a Gnostic way of thinking' such as we find later in the developed Gnostic schools of thought. In that respect the use of the term *gnosis* in a broad and comprehensive sense is legitimate and justified."[5]

It is just this *gnosis* outlook that we are now to observe as the object of Paul's critique in Romans 6. When the gospel was spoken in the hearing of first-century man, we must understand that the context within which he then thought, felt, and believed played a very important part in his ability to hear. Not only that, but Paul and the other New Testament writers faced on all sides what McL. Wilson terms these *gnosis* attitudes. Certainly there are even teachers (1 Cor.) who had already sought to bring the gospel of Christ under their own ideological control. It is against just this sort of attempt that Paul brings up his question of 6:1.

In the *gnosis* outlook only the spiritual has any real significance, since the body, the world, and the crisis of sin are only apparently real, and once the initiate knows (*gnosis*) the secret of spiritual energy, such matters as sin and ethics are left behind. Paul speaks to this issue. His answer is abrupt: "Shall we sin more to know more grace? By no means!"

I am maintaining that the question Paul asks in 6:1 "What shall we say then? Are we to continue in sin that grace may abound?" speaks more pointedly to persons within that Pre-Gnostic frame of mind than to legalists, whose problem is of the opposite nature.

Irenaeus writes some years later to describe the Gnostic ethical view of life as follows: "For as gold is cast into the dirt does not lose its beauty, but maintains its own nature . . . so they suffer no harm and do not lose their spiritual nature, by any acts at all which they do. Therefore, even the most perfect among them do, without fear, everything that is forbidden." Father Irenaeus should not be baffled by this because once everything is spiritualized things physical and actual such as ethics are unimportant. Now we are standing at the third crossroad.

"Do you not know that all of us who have been baptized into Christ Jesus were baptized into his death . . . so that as Christ was raised from the dead . . . we too might walk in newness of life" (6:3–4).

Redemption is not so much a medicine, or energy, as it is a new life and a new identity—we were baptized *into* Christ Jesus. Paul brings us back to the central part of the gospel. The Christian's hope is not placed in a transaction or a power but the person. The Christian good news is the "man" for the problem. Not only that, but the implications of that good news have to do with the reign of that man, the second Adam, in our daily lives. It is for this reason that we reject the option posed in the hypothetical question "shall we sin more?" We as Christians are not here dealing with laurel bark and sulphur fumes, like the oracle of Delphi, contriving crisis situations in order to test out narcotic religious effects. A far more important matter is at stake, and within this context Paul discusses the sign of baptism (6:3–11). Baptism is explained by Paul in a way which puts the most weight upon the event of baptism as the sign of the identification of the Christian with Christ. For Paul, baptism is not a heroic act on the part of the Christian believer nor does Paul show the slightest interest in ceremonial or liturgical procedures to be followed by the community of faith. He assumes that his readers understand what the word "baptism" means. For him, what is vital is the theological meaning of baptism as *identification* with Christ and therefore new *identity* for the believer. Consider each of these words.

(1) *Identification.* That which dominates the whole passage, 6:3–11, is the phrase *"into Christ Jesus."* He means that being a Christian involves our unique and individual ("all of us who have been . . .") relationship with Christ the one who died and was raised. Paul is teaching in this passage that baptism is the open acknowledgment and acceptance on the part of the Christian that the death and victory of Jesus is the event in my behalf. Baptism in this context is the Christian's answer to Romans 5:8, "God shows his love for us in that while we were yet sinners Christ died *for* us." By the sign of baptism the Christian, and the church along with him, gratefully replies, "The yes of faith in response to God's grace."

(2) *Identity*. Paul also points up the fact that to be identified with Christ means that the old self has died and a new
self now stands. In this passage the chief marks of that new
self are described by two words: *alive* and *free*. "We too
might walk in newness of life" (6:4). "We shall be . . .
united with him in a resurrection . . ." (6:5). "So you must
also consider yourselves dead to sin and alive to God in
Christ Jesus" (6:11). Free: "no longer enslaved to sin" (6:6)
"but freed from sin" (6:7). The result of our identification
with Christ, the new life that he grants in that identification,
is neither our escape out of the real world nor the loss of
our own humanity, but the discipleship of men and women
who *walk* here and now in newness of life. The force of the
first person pronoun "we" (6:4, 5, 6, 8, 9) and the subsequent
ethical teaching—"Let not sin therefore reign in your mortal
bodies . . ." (6:12)—makes clear to us that Paul is not
teaching that the concrete individual person is obliterated
or canceled out in his baptism into Christ Jesus.

Nor does baptism become the mystical journey out of the
world. Paul does not teach that we become gods or angels in
our baptism but instead "alive to God in Christ Jesus." Paul
never teaches or implies the deification of man. Martin
Dibelius in his book *Paul* makes the comment: "Paul had too
much of the Israelite inheritance, and was too much filled
with the Old Testament awe of the eternal God, to be able
to put himself, even for a moment, on the same plane as the
Lord of the world."[6] Dibelius goes on to observe that Paul
consistently avoids the Greek word *apotheosis*, literally
deification, in referring to man, though he can and does
speak of *newness of life* in Romans 6 and *transformation* in 2
Corinthians 5 and Romans 12.

We must now observe one further essential ingredient in
the Apostle's argument. The newness of life and the freedom
(which we will later consider in some detail) are both dependent upon two concrete events: the death and the resurrection of Jesus. When Paul speaks of man he will not speak
of phantoms but of real people ("Your mortal bodies . . .

do not yield your arms and legs to sin . . ." 6:12, 13). When
Paul speaks of Christ he has no phantom in mind either, but
the Jesus Christ who was put to death (4:25), who in fact
really died, "the death he died" (6:10) and who was "raised
from the dead" (6:4). Karl Barth has pointed out that as the
resurrection of Christ is a concrete event—the tomb was
empty—so also it is the happening for which there is no
historical precedent, unlike all other events, such as birth
and death. This is precisely why *proofs* for the resurrection
of Jesus are thwarted: one empty tomb is like every other
empty tomb. "In the invisible totality of the new man Jesus,
that is, in the concrete, corporeal person of the risen Jesus,
the direction in which his visible life had moved is re-
versed. . . . This reversal or transformation is not a 'historical event' which may be placed side by side with other
events. Rather it is the 'non-historical' happening, by which
all other events are bounded."[7] Barth's use of the term "non-
historical" is probably confusing, and I would use the term
"radical historical," since it seems to me that this phrase
better grapples with the angels' question of the women at
the tomb, "Why seek ye the living among the dead?" It is
this radical historical event which Paul establishes as the
foundation for Christian identity: "for we know that Christ
being raised from the dead will never die again; death no
longer has dominion over him . . . let not sin therefore
reign in your mortal bodies" (6:9, 12).

   Freedom is the word used by Paul to describe the Christian's new life. We now want to consider the passage 6:12–
7:6 in which the Apostle explains this word *freedom* and its
opposite *slavery*.

   We have already met the theological concept of freedom
long before the word appeared here in the text of chapter 6
and this fact was briefly noted in connection with 1:18–28
and in 5:12–21. The question which stands at the threshold
of chapter 6, "Are we to continue?" also rests upon a premise
that there are authentic choices for persons to make and

for which we bear the responsibility. Fatalism has no part in Paul's message to the Romans. The assumption of chapters 6 and 7 is precisely that the human being is called to form conclusions that lead to decisions—"critical moments."

The crisis has to do with freedom: "By his own bad choices man lost both himself and his freedom . . . therefore what matters most is not the free will of man but the will of man set free" (John Calvin).

In Paul's view the full impact of the grace of God (1:18– 5:21) is not the destruction of human will but rather the liberation (redemption) of man and his will. This is startling to the first-century ideological Greek who is conditioned to think of relationship with deity in terms of *eros* and not the New Testament coined word *agape*. He is one who expects and even longs for the overwhelming absorption of the human self as a result of contact with the "divine" so that all inhibition and ability to make decisions is swept away in the ecstasy of *eros*[8] Paul's language of freedom and authentic selfhood must sound strange, indeed, to such a person! The love of God has freedom and justice in it, whereas *eros* is the love demanded by beauty and power. God's love grants freedom, *eros* imposes ecstasy and abandon.

We now see the vital connection between *freedom* and *faith* in Paul's theology. In chapter 6 the Apostle specifically names the word *freedom* and in a decisive way, but the foundation for that discussion is the teaching on baptism which is the sign not only of God's all-sufficient grace but also of our trust in that very grace. It is that act of trust toward God which both demonstrates the freedom of the human being in decision-making and by which he begins the journey of freedom which we call discipleship.

Paul now explores the meaning of freedom by means of two prepositions, "from" and "to."

(1) Freedom *from* sin (6:7, 18, 22). Paul means by this phrase that the offenses that have cumulated into a vicious spiral have now by the mighty intervention of God been

defeated; therefore, this freedom from that spiral of fear and
hurtfulness is God's gift to man. God himself sets us free.

(2) Freedom from the Law is also taught by Paul in this
passage (7:3, 4, 6). Paul's use of "law" is indeed compli-
cated but may be understood when we keep in mind that he
is using the word in a twofold sense. First he refers to the
Law as that plumbline of God by which we have always
been judged. He also intends a second interpretation of law
as that way of life which was never able to create newness,
produce hope, reconciliation, or life. In other words, Paul
interprets law in this second sense, in terms of its crucial
shortcoming. Although the Law has been held over against
the warped and crooked foundations of man and his civili-
zations for centuries, it cannot of itself heal or mend or
straighten; it only mocks the inadequacies of men and their
children. Paul then goes on to make an obvious point in
7:1–6: God is the master builder who himself establishes the
righteous foundation so that the work upon the whole house
may get under way. In this sense the building is set free
from work stoppages caused by endless appeals to the Law
for measurement and evaluation.

(3) The preposition "to" completes the Apostle's description. Freedom *to believe* in God (6:13), freedom *to
live* (6:4, 13, 22), freedom *to yield* our whole selves to
righteousness, to sanctification (6:19, 7:4).

This is the language of identity expressing its fulfillment.
Paul is teaching that the Christian reaches his full stride as
a human being in God's sight only as he gets on with the job
of living out the purpose for which he has been redeemed.
"So that you may belong to another, to him who has been
raised from the dead in order that we may bear fruit for
God" (7:4).

Section 2—Romans 7:14–25—GRAND TENSION

7: 14)We know that the law is spiritual; but I am
carnal, sold under sin. 15)I do not understand my own

actions. For I do not do what I want, but I do the very thing I hate. 16)Now if I do what I do not want, I agree that the law is good. 17)So then it is no longer I that do it, but sin which dwells within me. 18)For I know that nothing good dwells within me, that is, in my flesh. I can will what is right, but I cannot do it. 19)For I do not do the good I want, but the evil I do not want is what I do. 20)Now if I do what I do not want, it is no longer I that do it, but sin which dwells within me. 21)So I find it to be a law that when I want to do right, evil lies close at hand. 22)For I delight in the law of God, in my inmost self, 23)but I see in my members another law at war with the law of my mind and making me captive to the law of sin which dwells in my members. 24)Wretched man that I am! Who will deliver me from this body of death? 25)Thanks be to God through Jesus Christ our Lord! So then, I of myself serve the law of God with my mind, but with my flesh I serve the law of sin.

These verses (7:14–25) compel the reader of Romans to struggle with some hard questions. First we must decide what Paul means to say in this autobiographical section, and then we must grapple with his message ourselves.

Is the Apostle speaking in a rhetorical sense? Or is he speaking personally from his own present experience? The second possibility, in that it takes the pronouns at face value, is the more obvious interpretation, which as a rule in biblical exegesis is the more preferred. It also harmonizes with what we know of Paul's writing style in other letters, Galatians and Corinthians in particular.

The more critical question, however, has to do with the actual intent of the Apostle's words: (1) When he tells of inner warfare, is he speaking of former days in his life before he trusted Jesus Christ for salvation? (2) Or is he sharing out of his Christian journey following salvation but prior to sanctification (the fullness of the Holy Spirit)? (3) Or is Paul telling of his journey as a Christian in the midst of sanctification?

The mixture of opinion and the reasoning by interpreters

throughout the history of the church is richly varied. Certainly the interpretive option that the reader chooses to follow will greatly affect his understanding of the entire third part of Romans and even more than that—Paul's doctrine of sanctification. A brief survey of the opinions of New Testament interpreters is important at this point.

(1) The nineteenth-century expositor Joseph Agar Beet writes in defense of option one. His argument is subjective. "There are thousands who with deep gratitude acknowledge that, while verse 22 describes their past, it by no means describes their present state. Day by day they are more than conquerors through him that loved them. And . . . it is to themselves an absolute proof that these words do not refer to Paul's state when he wrote the Epistle. For they are quite sure that what they enjoy the great Apostle enjoyed in still higher degree."[9]

Bultmann comes to the same position and writes with the same confidence: "It seems to me that sufficient discussion has been given to this problem. There can no longer be any doubt as to the answer. It is fundamentally the status of man under the Law which is characterized here, and that, as it is seen through the eyes of one whom Christ has freed from the Law."[10] Dr. Bultmann holds that Paul is writing the section 7:14–25 in a rhetorical sense in order to portray more powerfully the greatness of grace over Law. Emil Brunner also agrees, and therefore Brunner finds himself only able to understand the sentences 14–25 as a digression in Paul's argument. His commentary on Romans chapter 8 begins with these words: "The theme is indeed the same which has been under development ever since chapter 5, except, of course, for the great interruption in the seventh chapter."

(2) Some interpreters have taken the second option. Kenneth Wuest in his commentary on Romans presents the following overview: "The key word in Romans 6 is 'machinery.' Here we have the mechanics of the Spirit-filled life. . . . In Romans 8 we have the dynamics of the Spirit-

filled life. . . . In Romans 7 we see the monkey wrench, self-dependence, which when trapped into the inner workings of this machinery, stops the works. . . ."[11]

(3) The third option, in my view, is the one supported by the most persuasive evidence from the text itself, and which I believe also leads the interpreter on to the highest ground. Anders Nygren answers Bultmann's position as follows: "No it is not Paul, but his interpreters, who have attempted an abstraction. They start with an assumption as to the meaning of the Christian life. Beginning with the fact that the Christian has received the Spirit, they draw the inference that 'the flesh' no longer plays any role, so they describe the Christian life in terms that are not true to the actual situation."[12]

F. F. Bruce agrees: "This is no abstract argument but the echo of the personal experience. . . . Paul himself knows what it means to be torn this way and that by the Law."[13]

But the profoundest arguments come from the Reformers John Calvin and Martin Luther, both of whom struggled to understand the Apostle Paul in this very passage. John Calvin stands as the greatest biblical commentator of all time. His commentary on 7:14–25 rings as true in the twentieth-century discussion as it did during the Reformation. ". . . the whole, then, of this reasoning may be more fully and more distinctly understood, we must observe, that this conflict, of which the Apostle speaks, does not exist in man before he is renewed by the Spirit of God. . . . For regeneration only begins in this life; the relics of the flesh which remain, always follow their own corrupt propensities, and thus carry on a contest against the Spirit."[14]

Martin Luther comes to the same position as Calvin.[15] Luther states his understanding of Paul: "Now notice what I said above, that the saints at the same time as they are righteous are also sinners . . . are like sick men under the care of a physician; they are sick in fact but healthy in hope and in the fact that they are beginning to be healthy . . .

they are people for whom the worst possible thing is the presumption that they are healthy, because they suffer a worse relapse."[16]

We must now consider two themes that, taken together, integrate Paul's teaching: the first is Paul's view of the Christian person; the second, his view of the dialectical tension within which the Christian lives his life here and now. It soon becomes clear that only the person with faith in the integrity and love of God will dare to venture this discipleship of freedom to which the Apostle bears his own witness and dedicates his life.

Paul's view develops as follows: The Christian person, described in chapters 6 and 7:1–13 as the one with life and freedom, is a *real* person, historical, definite, with body and spirit. It is this person who is baptized and who in Christ is to bear fruit for God in the world. It is this real person who now admits to an inner battle at the very place where his life comes into contact with God's will and with the world. Later we will try to understand Paul's teaching concerning that battle, but at this point we must note that 7:14–25 sets the Christian person free from still another tyranny—a bondage as deadening as sin itself—that tyranny which Luther called the "presumption that I am flawless." The Christian is not papier-mâché but flesh and blood—body and spirit—yet this very one, this very person, is beloved of God (5:8). This is the Christian who faces a new crisis, the crisis on the side of grace. "I am carnal" (literally flesh, *sarkos*, 7:14). "Sin dwells within me" (7:17). "I see in my arms and legs (members) that is, my concrete self, another law at war" (7:23). "I delight in the Law of God, in my inmost being" (7:22).

It is a complex portrait that Paul sketches for the reader: "I serve the Law of God with my mind, but with my flesh I serve the law of sin" (7:25). Gnosticism resolved this inner complexity by an escape from the body through the discovery of spiritual breakthroughs. But even within the

Christian community, this whole view of man in Romans 7:14–25 has often been ignored. Both within Catholic and Protestant devotional aspiration, the theory has emerged in different forms that certain of God's saints are able or enabled to become perfected beyond the tension to which the Apostle Paul bears his own witness in these sentences. The result is a life in "harmony" and, therefore, progressively in less and less need of the forgiving grace of God. Christian sanctification in such a view means that, as the Christian truly grows, he needs less and less of the best gift—the forgiving love of God.

Protestant liberalism of the nineteenth and twentieth centuries "solved" Paul's crisis of the Christian life by simply washing out all reality of crisis at the outset, and conferring trouble-free spirituality to all. But the Book of Romans has haunted these efforts when the book is taken as it is and not subjected to reductionism. Karl Barth in his commentary on these verses decides to hurl the challenge of Paul against the great father of nineteenth-century liberalism himself, Friedrich Schleiermacher. Barth goes to the psychological core and compares Paul's anthropology to modern liberalism's glorified view of man: "If the law of my religious being and having, were itself Spirit; if sensitive 'apprehensions of the absolute,' 'feeling and taste for eternity' (Schleiermacher) could seriously be regarded as lying within the realm of human competence; if God and such a man as I am could be treated as co-partners . . . then I should be led on to describe and comprehend myself quite properly as the answer to the problem of life. . . . But facts are hard, and it is difficult to retain even this confidence for long. . . . Who then am I? for I stand betwixt and between, dragged hither by my desires and by my hates, and thither by my inability to do what I desire and by my ability to practise what I hate."[17]

The problem with liberalism's man, as with perfectionist man, is that he himself too quickly becomes his own gospel;

he becomes his own answer to the problem of life. But try as he may to be spiritual and sensitive to the divine, nevertheless the inevitable drift for him is toward autonomy, which he then, either arrogantly or ignorantly, celebrates as freedom. "But facts are hard, and it is difficult to retain confidence for long." Paul proposes a more healthy way in the realistic sentences of 7:14–25.

In Paul's theology this important text results in neither the glorification nor the brutal diminishment of man. Instead of these false options Paul offers the realism of the gospel of Jesus Christ. Observe Paul's language closely. He outlines the nature of man in terms of *body, flesh, mind, spirit* (7:18–8:10). He does not hesitate to discuss the crisis, the civil war, that harasses the Christian person with painful tensions within his very nature (7:14–25). See also 8:10; 8:18; 8:26; 12:3.

"Flesh and spirit wage incessant warfare the one against the other within the citadel of man's soul. This warfare, as described in Paul's writings, is not the warfare between matter and mind, between physical and rational elements in man, which we meet in Greek philosophy. The background of Paul's usage of these terms is the Old Testament."[18]

The above observation by Professor F. F. Bruce is of crucial importance. Paul writes of the battle of spirit and flesh in the context of the Old Testament understanding of man's nature. The Old Testament sees man as a totality of spirit, body, emotion, family, past history, future fulfillment —all united into one whole. The warfare of which Paul speaks is the battle within this biblical understanding of the whole man. ."Paul's characteristic antithesis of flesh and spirit is to be seen then as directed neither toward the contrast of transitory and everlasting nor towards the experience of withdrawal from an earthly to a heavenly state. This antithesis connotes rather the attitude of the man who is delivered over by the sin of disobedience to the powers of the world without thereby being lost to the true Lord."[19] Greek philosophy could not accept this total view, which is the reason the philosophers of Athens gulped with astonishment when Paul told them of the Christian hope of resurrection of the body (Acts 17). The Greek desire for the spiritualization of man—that is, the escape from the body—will eventually become the chief premise of the Gnostic "gospel" of redemption. But the Apostle Paul has already clearly broken with such aspirations in 6:4: "we too might *walk* in newness of life"—not soar into the sky but *walk* as real people on the earth. ". . . so now yield the actual parts of your body to righteousness for sanctification" (6:19). "So then I of *myself* serve the law of God with my mind . . ." (7:25). "I beseech you . . . to present your *bodies* . . . holy and acceptable . . ." (12:1). Each of these texts shows Paul's determination to keep the Christian person's life a here-and-now fact.

The question then for us now to face is this: How shall the Christian of Romans 7 actually live the Christian life here and now? Paul teaches that the Christian discipleship involves a grand tension between:

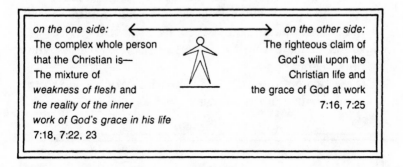

on the one side: ⟵　　　　　　　　⟶ *on the other side:*
The complex whole person　　　　　The righteous claim of
that the Christian is—　　　　　　　God's will upon the
The mixture of　　　　　　　　　　Christian life and
weakness of flesh and　　　　　the grace of God at work
the reality of the inner　　　　　7:16, 7:25
work of God's grace in his life
7:18, 7:22, 23

What Paul explains from his own experience in Romans 6 and 7 is that the Christian is one who faces up to this tension and then, trusting God (7:25, "Thanks be to God . . ."), throws himself into the battle. The Apostle thereby sets aside two false alternatives.

(1) Paul calls upon the Christian to reject all game plans for the Christian life that arrange victory by the shortening

of the race. One might conceivably argue that since grace
has set us free from law, "since you are not under law but
grace" (6:14), is it not sensible to argue that the demands
of God's law should be therefore accommodated to the
realities of the cultural milieu and the actual spiritual
strength of the participants of the race? Such a solution
to the problem of living the Christian life makes use of a
particular theory about grace to blunt, in effect, the real demands of the Law—as well as the even greater demand of
grace (Matt. 5, 6, 7). In this way the tension is diminished;
a theory of "grace" has dissolved for such a person the pressure upon him of the righteousness of the Law of God.

Paul resists this option as a false one: "What then? Are we
to sin because we are not under law but under grace? By no
means!" (6:15). "What then shall we say? That the law is
sin? By no means!" (7:7). "So the law is holy, and the commandment is holy and just and good" (7:12). "The law is
spiritual" (7:14). In Paul's experience of the Christian life
there is no escape from the tension with all of the stresses
that are involved. "Wretched man that I am!" (7:24).

(2) The Apostle also rejects the more subtle option which
would provide for an end to the tension of chapter 7 by the
elevation of man from the historical plane into the purely
spiritual realm.

These two options may be schematically described in the
terms of the diagram as follows:

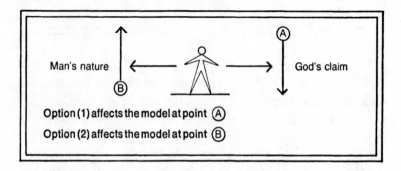

The question now is, How might this second option be accomplished?

The application of a mixture of first-century Greek philosophical premises regarding the nature of man together with carefully selected features of the Christian message of grace is the proposal that the Apostle increasingly is forced to grapple with throughout his ministry. "Man's soul is a particle of the divine breath, a spark of the divine fire . . . which Marcus Aurelius calls God within, king and lawgiver . . ." (John Ferguson). If such Greek aspiration is true, then man can be fully spiritualized either by death or by the interior plunge into divine secrets and flames that dwell within his own inner self, if only they can be discovered. Once this spiritualization is achieved, the grand tension between the claim of the holy God and the complexity of a whole man is resolved. It is "resolved" by the glorification of man. Paul always respects man but never indulges in such false glorification, and therefore this essentially Gnostic option is rejected. God is not the extension of man's ego in Paul's theology. The Apostle at all times preserves the full humanity of man, and it is therefore real men and women who must live the Christian life. That is the force of 7:14–25.

The glorification of man's spiritual inner-self as taught by early forms of Pre-Gnosticism and Proto-Gnosticism as noted earlier in this commentary are combatted throughout the New Testament (Corinthians, Colossians, Ephesians, 1 John, the Gospel of John, the Apocalypse, 2 Timothy, and now in Romans). What we find in chapter 7 of Romans is a powerfully moving confrontation against these emergent forms of the heresy which solves the grand tension by the spiritualization of Man–Spirit.

Two twentieth-century novels, the one a classic, the other a best seller, illustrate the point in contemporary terms. In Richard Bach's *Jonathan Livingston Seagull*, the solution to the question of meaning is basically Gnostic: the discoveries

of Jonathan Livingston Seagull from Chaing of the "numberless number," of the "truth" that a seagull is not an actual
bird with a measurable wingspan but an "idea." Freedom
then means the discovery of this *gnosis* (knowledge) and the
boldness to venture it. But in his redemption all concreteness
is discarded, which is the reason why the ethical passages in
Jonathan Livingston Seagull are unreal. Jonathan Livingston
Seagull loves the "spirit birds," not the real birds in the
midst of their concrete totality.

Alexander Solzhenitsyn, like Bach, also grapples with the
meaning of life, in *One Day in the Life of Ivan Denisovich*.
But the conclusions are different! Solzhenitsyn insists that if
meaning is to be found it must be found within *a real*
twenty-four-hour period in the routine life of an ordinary
man. Not only is he not an unlimited idea or numberless
number, but he is in fact a very concrete man who lives day
in and day out in a numbered barrack in a numbered Sibe-
rian prison camp and he himself bears a number. The message of hope to Ivan does not come in spiritualistic absorption or escapism, but from a fellow prisoner who suffers
under an even longer sentence than does Ivan; it is Alyosha
the Christian with his New Testament gospel. The model
for the evening talk between Ivan and Alyosha is found in
Brothers Karamazov in which Ivan and Alyosha struggle
through the same issue in their famous noontime dialogue.
The stunning point of Solzhenitsyn's book is that Alyosha
finds meaning for his life within the twenty-four-hour segments that we all live. This is the difference between the
Gnostic gospel and the Christian gospel.

Let us make one final observation about Romans 7:14–25.
The rejection of the two false options focuses our attention
upon the meaning of freedom in the Christian person. The
effect of either the reduction of the claim of God, or the
spiritualization of man, were either chosen, would be to rob
the Christian of freedom. The cheap grace of the first is self-
indulgence. It is the removal of all points of stress where a

person stands before the Law of God and must decide for himself what his own next step shall be. He does his own thing but he is not free, because genuine freedom means an answer has been found to the question of meaning here and now. There is no meaning for man where God's will has been subverted. Bonhoeffer put it unforgettably, "Cheap grace is the grace we confer upon ourselves . . . justification taught as a general truth . . . it amounts to the justification of sin."

Option two, were it chosen, also has diminished man's freedom by a faulty anthropology. Flattery does not increase freedom, because freedom must be founded upon truth. Man reaches his greatest stride, his most wondrous freedom, when he is fully aware of his humanity, not when he imagines that he is God, or demigod.

Section 3—8:1–17—THE HOLY SPIRIT

8: 1)There is therefore now no condemnation for those who are in Christ Jesus. 2)For the law of the Spirit of life in Christ Jesus has set me free from the law of sin and death. 3)For God has done what the law, weakened by the flesh, could not do: sending his own Son in the likeness of sinful flesh and for sin, he condemned sin in the flesh, 4)in order that the just requirement of the law might be fulfilled in us, who walk not according to the flesh but according to the Spirit. 5)For those who live according to the flesh set their minds on the things of the flesh, but those who live according to the Spirit set their minds on the things of the Spirit.

6)To set the mind on the flesh is death, but to set the mind on the Spirit is life and peace. 7)For the mind that is set on the flesh is hostile to God; it does not submit to God's law, indeed it cannot; 8)and those who are in the flesh cannot please God. 9)But you are not in the flesh, you are in the Spirit, if the Spirit of God really dwells in you. Any one who does not have the spirit of Christ does not belong to him. 10)But if Christ is in you, although your bodies are dead because of sin, your spirits are alive because of righteousness. 11)If the Spirit of him who raised Jesus

from the dead dwells in you, he who raised Christ
Jesus from the dead will give life to your mortal
bodies also through his Spirit which dwells in you.
    12)So then, brethren, we are debtors, not to the
flesh, to live according to the flesh—13)for if you live
according to the flesh you will die, but if by the Spirit
you put to death the deeds of the body you will live.
14)For all who are led by the Spirit of God are sons
of God. 15)For you did not receive the spirit of slavery
to fall back into fear, but you have received the spirit
of sonship. When we cry, "Abba! Father!" 16)it is the
Spirit himself bearing witness with our spirit that we
are children of God, 17)and if children, then heirs,
heirs of God and fellow heirs with Christ, provided we
suffer with him in order that we may also be glorified
with him.

The Christian lives his discipleship within the dialectical
tension described in chapters 6 and 7—at the center of the
tension between his own weaknesses and the uncompromised righteousness of God. At the close of these chapters
one question crowds all of the others to the side: *How then
is it possible really to be a Christian within such a tension
between the Holy claim of God and the weakness of the
disciple?* The answer to this question has already been
affirmed by the Apostle in chapters 1–7. In fact what could
well stand as the summary of the whole was written in
5:1–5.

    5: 1)Therefore, since we are justified by faith, we
have peace with God through our Lord Jesus Christ.
2)Through him we have obtained access to this grace
in which we stand, and we rejoice in our hope of
sharing the glory of God. 3)More than that, we rejoice
in our sufferings, knowing that suffering produces endurance, 4)and endurance produces character, and
character produces hope, 5) and hope does not disappoint us, because God's love has been poured into our
hearts through the Holy Spirit which has been given
to us.

What we find in chapter 8[20] is an expansion upon 5:1–5 in
the context of the grand tension portrayed in chapters 6 and

7. Consider the diagram we made use of earlier to understand the tension:

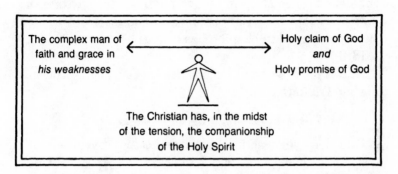

The diagrammatic scheme needs to picture the emphasis of chapter 8, God himself is our companion on the way. He journeys alongside of us in the twenty-four-hour experiences of our discipleship.

The third person in the Holy Trinity is mentioned in 5:1–5 in explaining the assurance of our salvation. Now in chapter 8 Paul will probe in more depth the doctrine of the Holy Trinity and the ministry of the Holy Spirit to the believer.

8:1–8. Paul's answer to the question, "How is it possible to live as a Christian in the real world?" has two parts: (1) It consists of an affirmation concerning the past tense (8:1–3). (2) It consists of an affirmation concerning the present and future tenses (8:4–8).

(1) Paul's first word of assurance has to do with the reality of God's resolution of human sin—man's existential past. The fact of the all-sufficiency of the redemption in Jesus Christ is repeated by Paul.[21]

(2) In verses 4–8 Paul asks his Roman friends to build actively upon the reality of the victory affirmed in 8:1–3. He calls for faith in God's decision. ("Set the mind on the Spirit.") Let me put it another way. Paul challenges the Roman Christians to live in the assurance of God's self-

revelation. In such a relationship the fulfillment of the Law
of God is made possible because of the grace of God. That
fulfillment takes place in and through our lives within, not
outside of the tension of chapter 7. (The reality of the tension is preserved in chapter 8 as well as chapter 7. See 8:10,
8:18, 8:26.)

At this point we want to consider Paul's teaching concerning our Trinitarian faith.

The Trinitarian Paragraphs 8:9–17, 26–27

Paul does not teach Trinitarian theology by means of a
systematic theological model, such as the Apostles' Creed
with its Article I, "I believe in God the Father. . . ." Article
II, "I believe in God the Son. . . ." Article III, "I believe
in God the Holy Spirit. . . ." These three articles of systematic theology have been very helpful for Christian teaching. Though the model is not found in the precise words of
the Creed in the Old Testament–New Testament documents; nevertheless the biblical witness fully supports the
formula. Here in Romans 8 the Apostle Paul adds his witness
to the total biblical portrait which the systematic theologian
must interrelate and interpret. What is it that Paul teaches
with relation to the nature of God in Romans as a whole and
here in 8:9–11 in particular?

(1) Paul teaches that God is father (8:16), creator
(1:25), almighty (1:20).

(2) Paul teaches the deity of Jesus Christ (8:32, 8:34,
8:39, and 5:10). These passages and others throughout the
book make use of various vocabulary forms to express the
uniqueness, lordship, power, authority, and divine nature of
Jesus Christ.

(3) Paul teaches God the Holy Spirit (8:9–17; 26–27).

There are two ways to describe this Trinitarian mystery of
the nature of God. One is to speak of the triune God in terms
of our own experience of the assurance of his character—
that is, how we have experienced God. The second is to seek

to find human words to describe the mystery beyond our own experience of God. Consider these two forms.

First we describe the triune God in terms of our experiences of his self-disclosure to us:

(A) Article (1), We believe in one God—Father, Creator, Almighty—the God of character (1:16, 17).

Article (2), Who has spoken for himself. This speech of God—the eternal word become flesh—is Jesus Christ, the Son of God (3:22; 5:1, 2).

Article (3), And who confirms that speech within the history of our lives—in this God is the Holy Spirit (8:16, 17).

(B) But it is not enough to describe the nature of God only in terms of our experience. There is also the objective mystery of the Godhead which is beyond human subjective experience. Within the very being of the eternal God there is love, fellowship, and relationship. This relationship is beyond human philosophical understanding, though psychologically we can hardly understand the reality of God's love apart from this inner fellowship within the very nature of God. The biblical evidence is found in the Gospels. We see the mystery in the prayers of Jesus, in the record of the ministry and witness to Jesus by the Holy Spirit. Jürgen Moltmann has written a theological study of the cross of Christ wherein he sees the trinitarian mystery decisively unfolded in the cross.[22]

Let us now consider in some detail the doctrine of the Holy Spirit. In the language of Romans 8:9–11, Paul makes use of a rich mixture of words to describe God the Holy Spirit. Note the words in order of appearance: "the Spirit," "Spirit of God," "Spirit of Christ," "Christ," "Spirit of him who raised Jesus," "he who raised," "through his Spirit." Spirit, *pneuma* (literally, "wind"), is related in this very compact paragraph to both Father and Son and is used in a single sense as well. Paul has deliberately constructed the paragraph in such a way that those who would set up a separate monism of the Spirit, or of Christ, or of God, the

Father, are thwarted in such attempts. One dilemma for
translators concerns the problem of knowing whether or not
to capitalize the word *Spirit* in each of its uses. "So fre-
quently in the following argument does the word clearly
refer to the Spirit of God that it is better to take it as referring to him throughout except where the context rules
this sense out. The human spirit is not excluded, however,
where the divine Spirit is understood. For Paul, the human
spirit is dormant or dead until it is aroused to life by the
Spirit of God."[23]

More precisely put, what do we mean in the description
of the Holy Spirit as the one who confirms the speech of
God within the history of our lives? ". . . It comes to this;
the Holy Spirit is the bond by which Christ binds us to
himself."[24] Within the sentences of Romans 8 the ministry of
the Holy Spirit is portrayed in just such terms. At each
crossroads in the text, he is the one who binds the believer
to the Savior—the Lord Jesus Christ. By means of the ministry of the Holy Spirit the Christians are made certain that
Jesus Christ is Lord not in a general sense but in their own
personal experience. I, as a simple Christian, may know the
love and authority of Jesus in my daily life, in terms of my
own existence. The fact that personal confirmation is possible is as the result of the ministry of the Holy Spirit. The
Spirit of God dwelling within the Christian believer is the
exact equivalent of Jesus Christ within the believer, "Christ
is in you. . . ." (8:9, 10). "Paul means, that the Spirit of
God gives us such a testimony, that when he is our guide
and teacher, our spirit is made assured of the adoption of
God: for our mind of its own self, without the assurance of
the Spirit, could not convey to us this assurance."[25]

John Calvin understands the crisis of chapters 6 and 7 and
sees its resolution too! The assurance that proves to the
Christian that he is in fact "making it" as a Christian is not a
dossier of his own successes with the law, his check list in
outdoing the Pharisees when it comes to righteousness, or a

log of mystic breakthroughs. The assurance that really sets him free is the inner witness of God's Spirit with his own spirit that he is a child of God. "You did not receive the spirit of slavery to fall back into fear, but you have received the spirit of sonship" (8:15).

What then is the test or proof of the fact that the "Spirit of God really dwells in you?" Paul's answer to this question is forthright and uncomplicated, "When we cry 'Abba Father!' it is the Spirit himself bearing witness with our spirit that we are the children of God" (8:15, 16). This means simply being assured enough of Jesus Christ and of his love that in spite of a thousand contradictions the Christian believes in Christ's love, choosing to trust Christ. The confirmation within our own selves, which we receive from the Holy Spirit, our guide and teacher, is proved by our ability to say "Father." *Abba* is an Aramaic word which means "father" in an affectionate, personal sense. (*Abba* is used in two other places in the New Testament, Mark 14:36 and Gal. 4:6).

Paul is teaching that only the Holy Spirit himself grants to the Christian such an assurance. Paul's teaching is not characterized with elaborations or further tests of the reality of this indwelling. On our side Paul calls for faith; that is, the willingness to trust in the witness of the Holy Spirit to my spirit and the willingness to be identified fully with Jesus Christ—"fellow heirs with Christ, provided we *suffer* with him." The word "suffer" is here used in the sense of the involvement of our whole concrete self with Christ in sorrow as well as joy.

Martin Luther draws a fascinating analogy which is very helpful at this point.

"*What the Law could not do*. The Apostle prefers to say 'What the Law could not do' rather than, 'What we could not do' even though the disability belongs to no one but to us, who were weak and unable to fulfill the Law. But he does this . . . for he is arguing primarily against those who trust

in the powers of their own nature and think that no other
help is necessary for righteousness. . . . The Apostle argues
against their empty faith in the Law. . . . In this the Law
is not at fault. . . . It is as with a sick man who wants to
drink wine because he thinks that his health will return if
he does so. Now the doctor should say to him, without any
criticism of the wine, 'It is impossible for the wine to cure
you, it will only make you sicker.' The doctor is not con-
demning the wine but only the foolish trust of the sick man
in it. For he needs other medicine to get well so that he then
can drink his wine."[26]

Luther's analogy speaks to our own contemporary situation. I remember a senior theological colloquium during my
own seminary days at Princeton Theological Seminary. Our
professor posed an apparently simple question to the sem-
inar, "Who is a Christian?" Our discussion for the first several minutes was completely under the sway of the current
bias of our theological generation; we described the Christian as the one with ultimate concern, as the one who dared
to care, as the one who boldly and prophetically challenged
the pretenses of a sick social order. The discussion con-
tinued in this direction with each definition more impressive
and dominant than the one before.

The neo-legalism of our discussion was finally exposed
when one student asked another question. "These definitions
are all activistic, but I want to ask this, Is your man or
woman a Christian when he is asleep?" His rejoinder exposed
our definitions for what they were—our own idealistic tests
of what would constitute for us a "real" Christian—that is,
our own "revolutionary" legalism. Whereas the legalistic
party at Galatia insisted upon the rite of circumcision as the
test of authentic fulfillment, we had updated the tests of the
Galatian sect with our own legalistic test—"Do you speak in
tongues?" "Do you have the gift of healing?" "Are you really
joined in the battle against racism?" "Are you prophetic?"
"Are you socially involved?" Each of these has its own

inner validity, but when they become the means of the assurance of salvation—and in some cases even become the
substitute for salvation itself—they are a perversion of the
gospel. Luther warns that we may desire wine to make us
well but the doctor rightly scolds us, "The wine will only
make you sicker." That is nothing against the wine but only
against the faith in the wine as the cure, when God has
granted his own cure. "(We) did not receive the spirit of
slavery to fall back into fear, but the spirit of sonship. . . ."

Legalism, whether it takes the form of a ceremony, a gift,
a concern, a theory, always has enslaved the Christian and
does not deserve to become the test of salvation or sanctification. Legalism—old or new—is unable to assure the believer
because only the Spirit of God himself enables us to say
Abba father as sons, no longer slaves.

Paul's teaching concerning the Holy Spirit is clear. The
Holy Spirit does not guide and teach the Christian into new
truths beyond the word of God, Jesus Christ. This would
amount to mysticism. But rather the Holy Spirit bears
witness with our spirits that the Speech already made by
God is sufficient. We Christians need nothing more than to
be heirs of God, fellow heirs with Christ. There are no
further "secrets" that await the Christian, who then by
the discovery of such secrets becomes somehow superior
to the rest of the brothers and sisters. Such a misunderstanding of the Holy Spirit's ministry has always been damaging
and has always produced a neo-legalism in the church.

In the paragraph 8:18–25 Paul speaks of "first fruits."
". . . but we ourselves, who have the first fruits of the
Spirit, groan inwardly as we wait for adoption as sons, the
redemption of our bodies" (8:23).

By this image (*aparche* is also used in Romans 11:16)
Paul shows that the ministry of the Holy Spirit in the
Christian's life is not an end in itself but points toward
the hope of the completed redemption of our bodies. Something of the same concept, though by the use of a different

Greek word (*arrabōn*) is used by Paul in 2 Corinthians 1:22,
5:5 and Ephesians 1:14 where he describes the ministry of
the Holy Spirit as a guarantee. "He has put his seal upon
us and given his Spirit in our hearts as a guarantee" (2 Cor.
1:22).

In all of this language, as is the case throughout the New
Testament teaching concerning the Holy Spirit, the emphasis
is upon the ministry of assurance by the Holy Spirit—the one
who comes alongside (2 Cor. 1) to authenticate within
ordinary men and women's lives the reality of Jesus Christ
as Lord and Savior.

Section 4—Romans 8:18-30—GOD'S DECISION

8: 18)I consider that the sufferings of this present time
are not worth comparing with the glory that is to be
revealed to us. 19)For the creation waits with eager
longing for the revealing of the sons of God; 20)for
the creation was subjected to futility, not of its own
will but by the will of him who subjected it in hope;
21)because the creation itself will be set free from its
bondage to decay and obtain the glorious liberty of the
children of God. 22)We know that the whole creation
has been groaning in travail together until now; 23)
and not only the creation, but we ourselves, who have
the first fruits of the Spirit, groan inwardly as we wait
for adoption as sons, the redemption of our bodies. 24)
For in this hope we were saved. Now hope that is seen
is not hope. For who hopes for what he sees? 25)But
if we hope for what we do not see, we wait for it with
patience.
26)Likewise the Spirit helps us in our weakness; for
we do not know how to pray as we ought, but the
Spirit himself intercedes for us with sighs too deep for
words. 27)And he who searches the hearts of men
knows what is the mind of the Spirit, because the
Spirit intercedes for the saints according to the will
of God. 28)We know that in everything God works
for good with those who love him, who are called according to his purpose. 29)For those whom he foreknew he also predestined to be conformed to the
image of his Son, in order that he might be the first-

> born among many brethren. 30)And those whom he
> predestined he also called; and those whom he called
> he also justified; and those whom he justified he also
> glorified.

God has decided, and everything in creation receives its
own meaning from the decision of its creator, God himself.
This is the thesis of verses 8:18–30. Over against this claim
Paul anticipates two questions:

(1) What is the place of the Christian in God's decision?

(2) How sure is the decision of God in the face of change,
decay, and other threats against it?

In Greek philosophy the world is an apparent reality; true
reality belongs to spiritual categories. Therefore, in such a
view history tumbles continually in upon itself in a cyclical
way without long-term meaning or goal. Meaning and final
purpose are always reserved for the spiritual reality; as a
consequence, the Greek view of man should in every way
possible find means of anticipating this higher reality by
escape from the present world order, from the body, from
history.

History might be portrayed as an enclosed circle-like
prison for man; but since man is partially spirit he is never
completely within the circle.

In Greek philosophy then, man, by virtue of his inner spiritual capacity, his divine flame, lives restlessly within earth-prison and yearns to be free from his own body and from history. The question is, How? Plato offered the conclusion which dominated Greek thought up to and including the Gnostic movement of the second century A.D. In the parable of the cave, Plato taught that it is the philosopher king who knows the difference between appearance and reality, and in that knowledge (*gnosis*) rests his true worth (salvation). Whereas lesser men were content with shadows, the philosopher king knows of the reality behind the shadows. For this reason he is in fact worth more than those content with shadows. By the first century the consensus in Greek thought was that all historical existence was in effect a shadow—even worse, a prison which through various deceptions held the spirit of man captive. Therefore, we can appreciate the search that was under way among Greek thinkers in the first century for means of escape from a rat-race world.

Robert M. Grant explains second-century Gnosticism in a way which helps us to see these Platonist longings now refined by the time of the second century and made religious, even quasi-Christian: "Gnosticism is a religion in which emphasis is laid on salvation for the spirit of man, a spirit divine in origin, submerged in evil matter, and rescued by virtue of recognition of its origin and nature. The recognition is the result of the knowledge provided by a redeemer–revealer who comes down from the spirit-world above and returns there. . . ."[27]

Salvation in such a world view is twofold: (1) spiritual actualization during the years of his own historical existence, and (2) at death his spiritual absorption into the higher ultimacy.

But the Old Testament speaks of man and history in a totally different way. In the creation narrative (Gen. 1–3) man is created in the sixth day of creation sharing the same

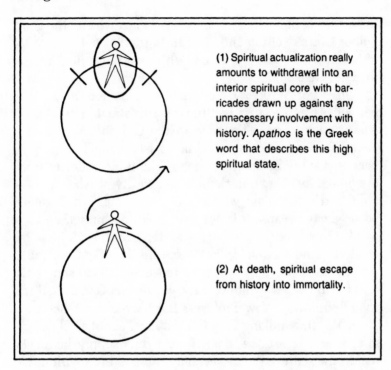

(1) Spiritual actualization really amounts to withdrawal into an interior spiritual core with barricades drawn up against any unnacessary involvement with history. *Apathos* is the Greek word that describes this high spiritual state.

(2) At death, spiritual escape from history into immortality.

day as most of the other living creatures. The seventh day is the day without ending, the day of ultimate fulfillment. But man is made in the sixth day—to be sure at the very edge, but nevertheless within the day that has an ending. In the Old Testament's theological understanding of man, he is not eternal—not even the spiritual part of him is eternal —but he is the one with dominion (freedom) on earth. He is privileged to name every part of the created order: animals, bacteria, stars, planets, the parts of his own body. Involved in that right to name is the right of dominance, but nevertheless, man, impressive as he is, is still mortal. "We start talking about the grace of God when we ascribe more to man than from dust to dust."[28]

In the Old Testament world of thought, the scandal of man is not the fact of his mortality and his identification with the creation, but rather his sin wherein he distrusts the good will of God's decision and arrogantly reaches out for means to become like God and to deny his own humanity. This is the fall (Gen. 3).

Man is not by creation ultimate, nor is there a spiritual part of his nature that is ultimate. He is man, and that is what he is meant to be. In both the Old and New Testaments, he never becomes God nor even an angel of heaven, because God wills that he be man. The Bible endorses fully the humanity of man in the full complexity of what he is— body and spirit. That which is ultimate, that which never passes away because it is not mortal, is God himself and his word. Only God is ultimate and the word by which he created. "And God said, 'Let there be light'" (Gen. 1:2). And the same word by which he redeemed: "God shows his love for us in that while we were yet sinners Christ died for us" (Rom. 5:8). Now Professor Barth's comment becomes clear. We start talking about God's love, about God's decision, when we ascribe more to man than simply his place within the sixth day. The meaning of man, both within the sixth day and by the grace of God within the seventh day, is dependent upon the decision of his creator–redeemer.

A whole new historical perspective emerges when we begin to understand the implications of this biblical view of man. It is radically different from that of Greek despair with its wheel-like repetition. The biblical view is dynamic, in that the freedom of man is reckoned with seriously; therefore, it is a real history of real people in real places, not shadows and caves. It is the story of people who really suffer and love, who fear, believe, and hope, and who are beloved by the Creator who made them. It is the story of the twenty-four hour segments and of God's love there.

Whereas the Greek view is a precise and mean circle, the biblical view is linear and complex; line upon line and interrelated. It contains the threads of faith and yet at the same time the threads of sin, of love and fear, small and large events. Within this scale the human reality is never really submerged in the cosmic vastness of it all because it is by God's decision that the human being has meaning—he is not the shadow or the analogy to some greater limitless number. Let me share still another diagram to portray the biblical view of historical existence.

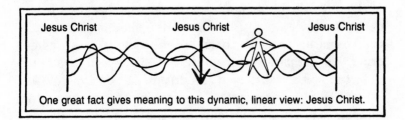

Jesus Christ   Jesus Christ   Jesus Christ

One great fact gives meaning to this dynamic, linear view: Jesus Christ.

(1) At history's beginning, standing before it, is the decision of God, "For in Christ all things were created, in heaven and on earth" (Col. 1:16).

(2) At history's decisive center is the word become flesh —the event Jesus Christ. "But now the righteousness of God has been manifested" (Rom. 3:21).

(3) Finally the same Lord Jesus Christ who is at the beginning and at the center of history stands also at its fulfillment. "When the perishable puts on the imperishable, and the mortal puts on immortality, then shall come to pass the saying that is written: 'Death is swallowed up in victory' . . . Thanks be to God who gives us the victory through our Lord Jesus Christ" (2 Cor. 15:54–57).

The Christian lives his life in the last times; that is, the time between the decisive center and the time of the eschaton, the fulfillment of history.

Paul paints a remarkable picture in 8:19–25 of this dynamic world view. He tells the Romans that the whole of the created order looks forward to God's fulfillment event, and that Christians (sons of God) are to play their role in that fulfillment. Paul teaches that the Christian and the historical

order of which he is a part—each of which is mortal—both
look forward, not to flight into the vague tapioca pudding
of spiritual escape but for the fulfillment of the *body*. The
platonic understanding of immortality is quite a different
matter. "Its immortality is conceived as some kind of absorption into universal mind, involving the elimination of everything which constitutes individuality. . . . The absorption
of the individual in the universe is only another term for its
destruction. . . ."[29] But Paul intends something more radical. He means that our concrete selfhood and the concrete
order that is a part with us in the first six days of creation is
to be fulfilled, not dissolved as a dream. The decision of God
is that the whole of creation has meaning. Presently we and
that whole order are confronted by the "bondage of decay,"
and nothing that man or matter can do changes or avoids
the yawning abyss of death. Whether they be pyramids, the
speculations of the philosophers, ecstasy or narcotic escape,
none of these have been successful in defying the mortality
of creation. Paul tells us that this abyss is not to our liking,
"not of its own will" (8:20). Nevertheless the mortality of
creation does not thwart God's decision, but is in fact a part
of that decision, though not the final part, "for the creation
was subjected to futility, not of its own will but by the will
of him who subjected it in *hope*" (8:20).

Here we have in Romans a further comment by the Apostle upon his doctrine of the resurrection. (See also the
theological summation to the famous sermon at Athens,
Acts 17 and 1 Corinthians 13.) Because of the actual victory
of Jesus Christ over death, sin, and the power of the devil,
this real world has worth in the most substantial sense.
"Therefore, my beloved brethren, be steadfast, immovable,
always abounding in the work of the Lord, *knowing that in
the Lord your labor is not in vain*" (1 Cor. 15:58). What
he means is that because of Christ's grace out of which the
world was made, because of the victory of Christ at the
decisive center, and because of Christ's ultimate fulfillment

of history, we who live now in this present dynamic, turbulent age, work hard not in fear or boredom but in hope. Not because night is coming and daylight is closing down, but because the day is coming (Rom. 13:12) we get on with the job God has called us to do (Rom. 8:28–30).

The New English Bible renders 8:28 as follows: "He [the Holy Spirit] pleads for God's own people in God's own way; and in everything, as we know, he co-operates for good with those who love God." In this translation the subject of the sentence 8:28 is the Holy Spirit (26, 27). The point is clear; it is the Holy Spirit who aids the Christian in his weaknesses, in his prayer, and in every experience of life.

It is important to note (1) what is taught and what is not taught in these often quoted two sentences, and (2) what is the nature of the aid that is promised.

(1) The passage does not adopt a fatalistic idealism toward the historical journey of the Christian. The text does not say that "everything is good" or that "everything is inevitable." Such views have the effect of negating the dynamic linear in favor of the bare single line linear. The

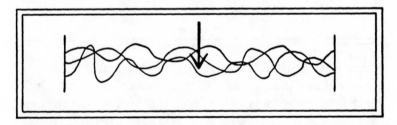

theological problem with such an idealistic, fatalistic view of the inevitable course of history is that both the *freedom*

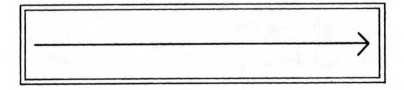

of man and the *freedom of God* are replaced by historical necessity. Marxism holds to this view of history. But in the Christian view, the one unchangeable reality is the decision of God. That decision is revealed in creation, redemption and the consummation (the Second Coming of Jesus Christ) of history. But the point is this: what we have discovered in *creation* and *redemption* is that God has decreed the freedom of man. The reality of this freedom of God and freedom of man plainly challenges the historical necessity taught by both Karl Marx and Plato. Note two views of historical necessity:

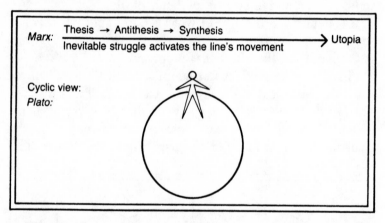

For Karl Marx, man is not in any sense spiritual, and he plays out his part primarily as a material and economic ingredient in the inevitable historical process of the struggle between classes. In Plato, man is glorified spiritually but devalued historically in that hope for mankind is viewed in escapist terms. It is the cyclic Greek view of history that Karl Marx rightly called an opiate meant to direct man's attention away from the historical line and toward "pie in the sky" spiritual release.

Paul's view of history is more turbulent and dynamic than that of Karl Marx and profoundly richer than that of Plato.

For Paul, God's decision is that man is real, that he does indeed possess dominion and that he is held responsible by God. He is in this sense free and therefore capable of gross sin with its destructive and brutal consequences. This freedom exists because of the sovereign decision of God and in the mystery of this freedom man is therefore able to believe, to love, to hope. Man is granted by God the possibility of the "critical moment," and he is not robbed of that moment. This is why salvation is not an automatic override of the human will, a triumphalism that destroys the genuineness of freedom by the irresistability of grace.

We must beware of all forms of idealism which, in order to make us happy, destroy the biblical view of who we really are. Universalism is one such theological disaster. We have the right and obligation to pray for the salvation of the whole world and then to trust in the justice of God's character; but it is quite a different story when we construct a theory which takes possession of God, confines his freedom into the box of our own definition of what his grace is or ought to be. It is far better to struggle theologically with the immense paradoxes of judgment and grace—sovereignty of God and authentic man—than it is to sweep away the struggle with a kindly theory about the future. Our resolution is not in the theory about history but in the Lord of history.

Creation and *redemption* have revealed to us the worth of man and the fact of his freedom. But what is more, they reveal the freedom of God as well. What we have discovered in the Bible is salvation by surprise, when we least expected it. Our freedom exists because of and only because of God's sovereign choice. We are free because he says so. History is real because God has willed it so. History is consummated and the last judgment is fulfilled as he chooses it to be and to happen. We are in the face of another essential dialectical tension. The biblical witness to God's grace and to man's faith preserves the dialectical nature of these two great facts: *the freedom of God by which he has decreed the freedom of man.*

Romans 8:28 does not teach that everything is good, because in fact many of the experiences of man are bad. But the promise that the Apostle makes is that in the midst of history, with its real tribulation, God enables his people (the text is plural) to take hold of events as they are in the assurance of Christ's Lordship over history. The aid that is promised to the Christian community is the strength to work with the Holy Spirit as our companion within the real history where our lives now journey within twenty-four-hour segments. Here is, therefore, no fatalism but a bold encouragement to the Christians at Rome to look for new chances in every old–new situation, to seize upon hope over against despair, to be assured that the Lord is with them every step of the way as he promised he would be. "Lo I am with you always. . . ."

Now in 8:29 Paul introduces the word "decision." The atmosphere of this famous sentence is missional, evangelistic. God has decided ahead of time (predestined) that those very Christians at Rome are to live out their Christian discipleship in order that many other people who journey alongside of their lives may be won to Jesus Christ the Lord. Paul concludes the sentence with the affirmation that the Lord of history is the one who brings his work to completion. "He who began a good work . . . will complete it" (Phil. 1:6). It is hazardous to develop a theory of divine election from this single sentence, especially in view of the contextual purpose of the passage. The Apostle is explaining to the people of God that they were called by the pre-decision of God himself *in order that* they might share the kingly reign of Jesus Christ with their neighbors—"many brethren." In this passage, that missional purpose is the context of Paul's statement. Paul wants his Christian brothers and sisters to know the fact that it is God himself who made the decision long ago that the world should be blessed because of a people blessed (Gen. 12:1–3).

Section 5—Romans 8:31–39—GOD IS FOR US

8: 31)What then shall we say to this? If God is for us, who is against us? 32)He who did not spare his own Son but gave him up for us all, will he not also give us all things with him? 33)Who shall bring any charge against God's elect? It is God who justifies; 34)who is to condemn? Is it Christ Jesus, who died, yes, who was raised from the dead, who is at the right hand of God, who indeed intercedes for us? 35)Who shall separate us from the love of Christ? Shall tribulation, or distress, or persecution, or famine, or nakedness, or peril, or sword? 36)As it is written, "For thy sake we are being killed all the day long; we are regarded as sheep to be slaughtered." 37)No, in all these things we are more than conquerors through him who loved us. 38)For I am sure that neither death, nor life, nor angels, nor principalities, nor things present, nor things to come, nor powers, 39)nor height, nor depth, nor anything else in all creation, will be able to separate us from the love of God in Christ Jesus our Lord.

"Who is against?" We know from 2 Corinthians 4 and throughout the biblical witness that indeed the devil is against us just as he is against God. But Paul decides in these amazing summary sentences to sweep aside every threat that may undo us in view of the greater power that is in our favor: "God is for us." Only four words, a sentence that may be spoken with four distinct emphases. *God* is for us. God *is* for us. God is *for* us. God is for *us*.

This paragraph begins with rapid-fire questions that are then followed by emphatic answers. The effect is electrifying! Paul's spare use of words, the sweep of thoughts that each short phrase brings to the mind of the reader makes this text a classic in the Greek language. The text is prose of superb style and inner force.

The themes in the text are not new to Romans 1–8, though

the imagery and word choice are new. Several key words make their first appearance in the Book of Romans here at this point: "who did not *spare*," "*elect*," "who shall *separate*," and "*tribulation*." There are deeply moving allusions to the Old Testament, "who indeed intercedes" (Isa. 53:12). Paul also quotes Psalm 44:22 applying the psalm to the experiences of his first-century Christian contemporaries.

One commanding theological point that the Apostle makes which he had not yet stated in Romans 1–8 is his teaching that the only one worthy to condemn (ultimately judge)— that is, who has the right to speak the last word of judgment —is Christ himself. The judge, the only judge, is Christ Jesus, the one who died and now reigns; who in fact is our advocate. These concepts are taught as inseparable facts about the Lord Jesus Christ throughout the New Testament (Luke 3:15–17, 1 John 1). This reference to judgment in the paragraph 8:31–39 establishes the eschatological nature of the passage. The great emphasis of chapters 1–8 up to this point has been primarily concerned, in a theological sense, with historical events: (1) the crisis of man's sin and the daily judgment (1:18–24) that man experiences because of sinfulness; and (2) the historical–ultimate event of God's act in Jesus Christ which grants to mankind the gift of redemption. Now there is a subtle shift in verbal tense. In these sentences the Apostle projects our attention toward the future. The present tense is very much his concern but it is the "present" within the eschatological time frame. This paragraph deals with the existence of the Christian in the last days, as history journeys toward the Second Coming of Jesus Christ, "who comes to judge the living and the dead."

There are no clues nor is there any discussion of the timing of the Lord's return. The position that the Apostle takes is that it is enough for us to know that the same Jesus Christ who stands at the origins, who died and rose again at the center, is the Lord who reigns in these last days

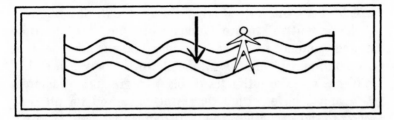

and in whose hands our lives are held at the end of history.

History is not a shambles of confusion and cross-purposes emptying into the inky abyss of nothingness. History moves toward the Lord who is the same yesterday, today, and forever.

Paul addresses the historical present in these verses 31–39 in the context of the judgment and redemption of Jesus Christ at the historical end. The reality of judgment is not, in Paul's view, swallowed up by grace but exists alongside of grace. Paul poses for the reader a wondrous paradox: the one who is judge is the one who has suffered all the punishment of judgment in our behalf.

Finally Paul affirms that in the face of the alarming and wholesale perils of the Christian's daily existence, the faithful love of Jesus Christ remains unwavering. Because of that love Paul predicts in superlative language—"more than conquerors"—that here in the real world the Christian should expect victory. Paul expects it. He does not despise his historical existence, even in view of tribulation or distress. Paul anticipates the victory of the gospel with ups and downs, not because of the greatness of the gospel's warriors but because of the Lord of the gospel, Jesus Christ himself. It is the love of Jesus that prevails.

This passage is an unforgettable example of the New Testament's eschatological context for the daily Christian life. Because of hope, the Apostle, and with him countless of the first-century Christians, were all the more active and bold in claiming ground here and now for the gospel. Authentic hope does not lead to daydreaming and wistfulness for Paul, but instead *hope* disarms the debilitating fear of the present and future. Hope enables the Christian to be strategic and not fanatical. "The moral fanatic imagines that his moral purity will prove a match for the power of evil."[30] Paul has no false estimates of his own greatness. Chapters 6, 7, and 8 have settled that issue once and for all. The secret to the strength of the Christian is that Jesus Christ is Lord. *Therefore* he calls out to the Christian, Let us abound in the work of the Lord, knowing that in him our work is not empty.

Part 6

Israel—Old and New

A Preface

The most important guideline in understanding Romans 9, 10, and 11 is to keep the three chapters united in interpretation. These chapters are complex and there are unmistakable paradoxes that emerge within the text like great independent pillars. That which unites the pillars into the same building is the foundation stonework of God's sovereignty—his own decision and trustworthiness. Freedom, responsibility, faith, and grace, are maintained in the end, each one with its integrity intact, and not at the expense of the other. In these three chapters Paul writes from the standpoint of past, present, and future. As theologian–historian, Paul interprets past and present. As revealer of the mystery of God's plan, he integrates the three time frames in terms of the future goal of God's will for both Israel and the non-Jewish world.

Let me offer a diagrammatic portrayal of the main features of the three chapters.

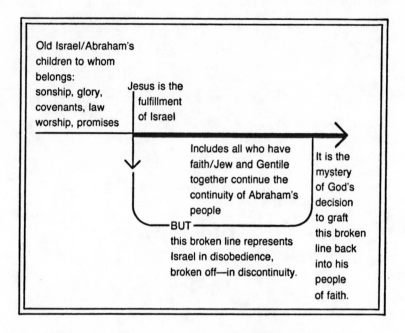

Old Israel/Abraham's children to whom belongs: sonship, glory, covenants, law worship, promises

Jesus is the fulfillment of Israel

Includes all who have faith/Jew and Gentile together continue the continuity of Abraham's people

BUT this broken line represents Israel in disobedience, broken off—in discontinuity.

It is the mystery of God's decision to graft this broken line back into his people of faith.

Section 1—9:1-5—THEY ARE ISRAELITES . . .

9: 1)I am speaking the truth in Christ, I am not lying; my conscience bears me witness in the Holy Spirit, 2)that I have great sorrow and unceasing anguish in my heart. 3)For I could wish that I myself were accursed and cut off from Christ for the sake of my brethren, my kinsmen by race. 4)They are Israelites, and to them belong the sonship, the glory, the covenants, the giving of the law, the worship, and the promises; 5)to them belong the patriarchs, and of their race, according to the flesh, is the Christ. God who is over all be blessed for ever. Amen.

Chapter 9 begins with Paul's introduction of Israel. He draws together the threads of the people's identity in the Old Testament by the use of six descriptive terms and two personal references: Paul tells us that to Israel belong: *the sonship, the glory, the covenants, the giving of the Law, the worship, the promises.* There are two personal legacies that he notes as also belonging to Israel: the *patriarchs*

(Abraham, Isaac, Jacob) and *Christ*, according to the flesh. What does he intend by this description?

Paul has poetically drawn together the story of the people of Israel by means of these words that tell of their *relationship* with God (sonship, covenants, worship, promises); in words that tell of their *experiences* as God's people (glory, giving of the Law, worship). He tells of the people's *hopes* (the promises). He tells of their *sources* (the patriarchs, covenants, Law). He tells of the *demands* made by God upon them (covenants, Law). He tells of their *traditions* (worship, glory). Finally he tells of their *fulfillment* (Christ). The Apostle does not methodically define each of the words that he chooses to depict the Old Testament history of Israel. For instance, he does not list the covenants that he has in mind. His purpose is different; his list is meant to stir up the reader to appreciate how great is the legacy of Israel. The list, much like Paul's lists in other places, does not propose to exhaust all that could be said on the subject. (Note Paul's list of spiritual gifts, Rom. 12:6–8, or his list of sins, Rom. 1:29–32.)

The true fulfillment of Israel is, "The Christ. God who is over all be blessed for ever. Amen" (9:5). In the diagram this fulfillment is pictured by the vertical intersecting line.

Section 2—9:6–13—THE FIRST PARADOX

9: 6)But it is not as though the word of God had failed. For not all who are descended from Israel belong to Israel, 7)and not all are children of Abraham because they are his descendants; but "Through Isaac shall your descendants be named." 8)This means that it is not the children of the flesh who are the children of God, but the children of the promise are reckoned as descendants. 9)For this is what the promise said, "About this time I will return and Sarah shall have a son." 10)And not only so, but also when Rebecca had conceived children by one man, our forefather Isaac, 11)though they were not yet born and had done nothing either good or bad, in order that God's purpose of election might continue, not because of works

but because of his call, 12)she was told, "The elder
will serve the younger." 13)As it is written, "Jacob
I loved, but Esau I hated."

Paul insists upon the radical intersection in Israel's history.
Jesus Christ is not another of the prophets or kings to be
included in an overall context of the nation Israel. Jesus
Christ is the radical fulfillment of the whole of Israel, and
therefore it is Israel that must now discover *its* meaning in
the greater whole of God's word and work: Jesus Christ. The
diagram must, in view of this intersection, portray the line
that continues following the event of Jesus Christ in history
as not an enlarged line, since Gentiles have been included,
but as a new line.

Here is the first of the paradoxes of Romans 9, 10, and 11.
On the one hand the continuity with Abraham, David, and
Moses is unbroken, yet the newness of that fulfillment is so
wholescale that old Israel must itself now be fitted into the
new reality by faith. Israel must trust in this fulfillment and
obey the claim of God's authority in Christ. If Israel does not
trust in Jesus Christ, her Lord, that denial amounts to the
rejection of the very fulfillment of the Old Testament people.
The result of unbelief is discontinuity for that part of Israel
which does not believe in God's word. The discontinuity
is represented by the break in the line and the formation
of a new one discontinuous with the Abrahamic line.

Paul's argument in 9:6–33 is that the question of Abrahamic succession is not to be settled by blood or tribal
ancestry but by the *promise* made to Abraham and by *faith.*
That is, God's decision and our human response.

The word "elect" was first introduced to the reader in
Romans 8:33. Now in 9:11 the word "election" appears
again. The concept of election in these sentences from Paul,
which include numerous references to Old Testament narratives and support quotations from the Old Testament,
establishes for the reader a second paradox. This is the
paradox between *the right to decree, which is alone the*

prerogative of God, and *the essential response of faith on the part of man.* This is so vital that Israel loses its very linkage to the promises of God if it does not "pursue through faith" (9:32). "But that Israel who pursued the righteousness which is based on Law did not succeed in fulfilling the Law. Why? Because they did not pursue it through faith. . . . They stumbled over the stumbling block" (9:32, 33). What an irony! The very fulfillment of Abraham's promise is found to be a stumbling block to Abraham's people! Paul sketches in these verses the lines of the paradox in a way which leaves no doubt that he is aware of the stress that each side of the polarity exerts upon the other: If God elects, why is man free? Why is he held accountable?

The Apostle has discussed Abraham in other places; in fact, no Old Testament figure receives as much theological evaluation from Paul as does the figure Abraham. To the Galatians Paul writes, "Thus Abraham 'believed God, and it was reckoned to him as righteousness,' so you see that it is men of faith who are the sons of Abraham. And the Scripture, foreseeing that God would justify the Gentiles by faith, preached the gospel beforehand to Abraham, saying, 'in you shall all the nations be blessed.' So then, those who are men of faith are blessed with Abraham who had faith" (Gal. 3:6–9). Paul has made his thesis clear in the Galatian text. Now he verifies that interpretation of Abraham once more and places emphasis upon the sovereign choice that God has made in his promise to Abraham and to Abraham's descendants, the choice revealed in Jesus Christ. Paul rules out every argument against God's radical intersection of the history of Israel. He reminds his readers that God is able to make his own decisions. This is the force of the Old Testament references to Jacob and Esau, to Pharaoh, and to Moses (Rom. 9:8–18).

And yet, though God makes his own choices, decisions that in no sense are dominated by men or by tribes, this very God has made "faith" the real possibility for men.

Faith is the crucial option for Israel, and for the Gentiles too. The word and event—Jesus Christ—is a stone across *every* man's path; it is a gateway that demands a decision from all who confront it; there it stands—either foundation rock or stone of stumbling; we cannot imagine that the stone does not exist. Romans 9:1–33 is a freedom text, and the closing Old Testament quotation (Isa. 28:16) seals the theological theme. God's choice enables man's choice; it is not possible for men to please God apart from the faith that chooses. Even Abraham's children who have such a rich legacy and heritage (9:4) must choose the very fulfillment of their own journey.

There is no such thing in Paul's theology as salvation taught as a general truth. God is the potter and we are the clay, but the clay that is man is some clay! "Man-clay" is the creation confronted with both testing and decision. These two inexorable parts of the whole paradox must be held together in the passage. John Calvin in commenting on the word "mercy" (9:23; 11:32) caught the significance of the paradox: "There is an emphasis on the word mercy; for it intimates that God is bound to no one, and that he therefore saves all freely, for they are all equally lost. But extremely gross is their folly who hence conclude that all shall be saved. . . . It is indeed true that this mercy is without any difference offered to all, but every one must seek it by faith."[1]

Section 3—9:33–10:4—FULFILLMENT

> 9: 33)As it is written, "Behold, I am laying in Zion a stone that will make men stumble, a rock that will make them fall; and he who believes in him will not be put to shame." 10: 1)Brethren, my heart's desire and prayer to God for them is that they may be saved. 2)I bear them witness that they have a zeal for God, but it is not enlightened. 3)For, being ignorant of the righteousness that comes from God, and seeking to establish their own, they did not submit to God's righteousness. 4)For Christ is the end of the law, that every one who has faith may be justified.

The rock in Zion is Jesus Christ. Paul teaches in this passage that the law is completed in Christ (10:4). The word "law" seen in this passage is held in tandem with the prophetic reference of 9:33 and is used in its wider connotation to include the whole of the Old Testament witness.

Paul quotes Isaiah 28:16 and Isaiah 8:14 in an interpretive way.[2] He makes decisive use of the Isaiah passages to press forward his major thesis of chapter 10 that both Jew and Greek (10:12) must make choices of either belief or unbelief in terms of that very stone in Zion. For Paul, the stone does not refer to a building or temple, nor by the word "Zion" is the prediction of the prophet meant to be an event concerning Jerusalem alone. As Paul sees it, the prophecy was the prediction that God's act at Zion would so take by surprise the expectations of the people that the stone would become the hope of the people, yet also it would divide the people. It was to cause some to stumble upon the event at Zion while others would trust in the event. The stone is too vast, too primary, too awkward to conform to former expectations and kingdom guidelines. Paul states in 10:3 that this stone is the righteousness of God revealed. The fact that a stumbling occurs points up the radically new nature of God's act in Zion. The Gospel narratives preserve this same note of surprise. John the Baptist, like his contemporaries, is also startled by Jesus (Luke 3:7); Jesus will not conform to even so great an expectation as John's.

Paul's most strategic sentence is 10:4, "for Christ is the end of the law. . . ." *Telos* may be translated "goal, termination." By means of the Isaiah quotation coupled with the 10:4 statement concerning the law, Paul makes his thesis clear: Jesus is the goal of the Old Testament; all Old Testament expectation and revelation now converge in him. Jesus completes the Abrahamic journey (4:16); he is the goal of the law (10:4); he is the everlasting Davidic king (1:3, 4); in Jesus the words of the prophets come to their goal (9:33).

Let us examine the prophetic fulfillment Paul claims in this passage. Earlier in this commentary I diagrammatically in-

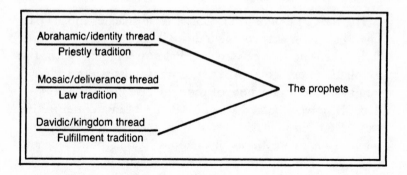

terpreted the theology of the Old Testament in terms of threads/themes/experiences that are held together and interpreted by the prophets of Israel.

The prophets spoke to the people on behalf of God, and for the people as representatives of their own generation. The prophets handled the threads of Jewish experience roughly, yet not as outside historical observers but as those who were themselves struggling from within to hear and obey God's word. The prophets were in continuous tension with the priests who represented the cultus and tradition of heritage (Abrahamic). The prophets also were in tension with the kings, even David himself (Nathan), who represented the fulfillment aspiration. It is the law of God which the prophets held over against king and priest, against false prophets and scribes of the law, and even the people at large. "The priests did not say, 'Where is the Lord?' Those who handle the law did not know me; the rulers transgressed against me" (Jer. 2:8).

What role then did the Old Testament prophets play in Israel? They were participants in the events. They were historians with a point of view. They were preachers who spoke and wrote to their generation. In most Old Testament passages the judgment–hope prophecies are portrayed together within the same contextual setting.

The Apostle Peter, as recorded by Luke in the Pentecost

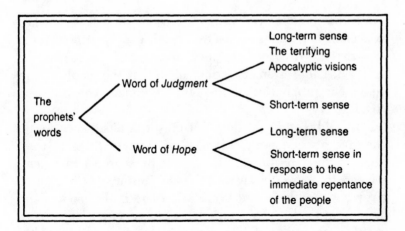

Day sermon (Acts 2:14–36), quotes a prophetic text (Joel 2:28–32) that exemplifies the mixture within one single prophecy of catastrophic judgment—"blood and fire, the vapour of smoke; the sun shall be turned into darkness and the moon into blood"—and the long-term hope of God's mighty act in behalf of men—"I will pour out my spirit upon all flesh and it shall be that whoever calls on the name of the Lord shall be saved." Peter claims that these prophecies, *both of them,* the word of hope and the word of judgment, are fulfilled in the cross and resurrection of Jesus of Nazareth. It is Jesus who has taken upon himself the overwhelming judgment predictions of Joel, Daniel, Ezekiel, and others. John the Baptist, the last of the great prophets of Israel, had predicted that Christ would "clear his threshing floor . . . and burn with unquenchable fire" (Luke 3). But no one, neither John nor the twelve disciples, were prepared to understand *how* the fulfillment of the wholescale judgment texts of John the Baptist and the other great prophets would take place. It is not *they,* the sinners, the oppressors, who die for six hours on Good Friday; it is *Jesus.* Jesus Christ took the catastrophic judgment upon himself unto death. J. S. Bach in his *Passion According to St. Matthew* identifies with the disciples and the echoes that they must have felt: "Ah

Golgotha, unhappy Golgotha . . . now who will the world's redeemer be?" Peter claims that death could not hold Jesus but that he disarmed, fulfilled, terminated (*telos*), every terror of Old Testament judgment so that the whole of the judgment prophecies of the Old Testament converges at Mt. Calvary.

The Old Testament does not only contain the awesome message of judgment: "Many shall stumble thereon, they shall fall and be broken; they shall be snared and taken" (Isa. 8:15); also, throughout the Old Testament, in Psalms, Proverbs, prophets, and historians, there is the longing for help from God: "The people who walked in darkness have seen a great light for the yoke of the burden, the rod of his oppressor thou hast broken" (Isa. 9:2 ff.). The Old Testament yearning for hope is expressed in profoundly rich and various ways: in personal terms (Ps. 57), in the language of the nation (Isa. 9:7), in aspirations for the city of Jerusalem and the temple (Ezek. 40:5 ff.).

The theological significance of the word *telos* (Rom. 10:4) is total and sweeping. Paul is saying that the hopes and the fears of the Old Testament—all of them—reach their goal in Jesus Christ, the stone in Zion.

Christ, by the cross and the resurrection, has conquered the power of death, sin, and the devil.

The victory of Christ is a total surprise to the expectations of Israel. It is hardly what either the Pharisees or the disciples envisioned! Paul autobiographically shares with the Philippians his own experience concerning that surprise (Phil. 3:3–11). At first Paul stumbled too.

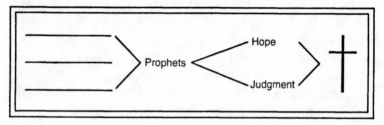

Serious biblical students today must be careful themselves not to stumble upon the stone in Zion by the establishment of our own theoretical–prophetic interpretations of the Old and New Testament documents in such a way that the *telos* is shifted from Christ to some other place. For example, it is a fact that both non-evangelical and evangelical Protestantism has been tempted to stumble into this error. Nineteenth-century liberalism so idealized man that he himself becomes the *telos* of the Old Testament prophetic aspiration for kingdom. On the other hand, certain prophetic movements within evangelical Christianity are endangered by a different sort of error. Dispensationalism[3] has developed an elaborate, highly creative, prophetic scheme which interprets many of the Old Testament hope and wholescale judgment prophecies as not yet fulfilled. The result is that Jesus Christ himself is diminished, not as in liberalism by the glorification of man, but in this case diminished by the plan of the ages, the prophetic unraveling. The further irony occurs as Christians with prophetic charts and schemes concerning the timetable of Jerusalem and the Temple find themselves with a theory that controls even the Second Coming of Jesus Christ himself. "In all that Paul says about the restoration of Israel to God (Rom. 11:25, 26), he says nothing about the restoration of an earthly Davidic kingdom, nothing about national reinstatement in the land of Israel. What he envisaged for his people was something infinitely better."[4]

Section 4—10:5–21—DISCONTINUITY

10: 5)Moses writes that the man who practices the righteousness which is based on the law shall live by it. 6)But the righteousness based on faith says, Do not say in your heart, "Who will ascend into heaven?" (that is, to bring Christ down) 7)or "Who will descend into the abyss?" (that is, to bring Christ up from the dead). 8)But what does it say? The word is near you, on your lips and in your heart (that is, the word of faith which we preach); 9)because, if you confess with your lips that Jesus is Lord and believe in your heart that God raised him from the dead, you will be saved. 10)For man believes with his heart and so is justified, and he confesses with his lips and so is saved.

11)The scripture says, "No one who believes in him will be put to shame." 12)For there is no distinction between Jew and Greek; the same Lord is Lord of all and bestows his riches upon all who call upon him. 13)For, "every one who calls upon the name of the Lord will be saved." 14)But how are men to call upon him in whom they have not believed? And how are they to believe in him of whom they have never heard? And how are they to hear without a preacher? 15)And how can men preach unless they are sent? As it is written, "How beautiful are the feet of those who preach good news!" 16)But they have not all heeded the gospel; for Isaiah says, "Lord, who has believed what he has heard from us?"

17)So faith comes from what is heard, and what is heard comes by the preaching of Christ. 18)But I ask, have they not heard? Indeed they have; for "Their voice has gone out to all the earth, and their words to the ends of the world." 19)Again I ask, did Israel not understand? First Moses says, "I will make you jealous of those who are not a nation; with a foolish nation I will make you angry." 20)Then Isaiah is so bold as to say, "I have been found by those who did not seek me; I have shown myself to those who did not ask for me." 21)But of Israel he says, "All day long I have held out my hands to a disobedient and contrary people."

What could be "infinitely better" than Zion restored? Paul now discusses the answer to that question. The Apostle mixes together two Mosaic references: Leviticus 18:5 in Romans 10:5 and Deuteronomy 30:12–14 in Romans 10:6–8. By means of these texts he establishes the underpinning for his earlier affirmation (Rom. 3:21–26) that what God requires of man is *faith*. Paul's specialized use of the Deuteronomy passage further supports the fulfillment emphasis just noted in the commentary on 9:33–10:4. Paul's point is that there is no way that we are able to "ascend into heaven" in order to uncover the Lord of the heights. He also asserts that there are none among us with the power to win the battle against death that only the Son of God himself can win. In the place of each option we are called upon to trust in the speech of God—the self-disclosure of God which is being preached in the gospel.

Verses 9 and 10 consist of an evangelistic formula, which Paul may be quoting in view of its use among the Christians. He fully concurs in the formula and states it in order to clarify the meaning of Christian faith. The formula defines faith as man's reply to God's act. God has spoken in Christ and now faith in the very basic and uncomplicated human answer to his speech, We believe and we confess out in the open that Jesus is Lord, that Jesus lives. Paul then assures the reader that this decision on our part to accept the Lordship of Christ and to trust in his victory; this faith results in our salvation. The word to "save" literally means to make safe, to salvage. "Total help for total need."

The Christian is one who has bowed twice: "once in humble admission that he is not autonomous, and again in humble gratitude to God for salvation in Jesus Christ" (Francis Schaeffer). The Apostle Paul is calling upon Jew and Greek to bow twice in just the same way.

Verse 10 states the assurance of salvation in terms of Hebrew parallelism, which gives support to the possibility that indeed Paul may be quoting an evangelistic faith formula of the apostolic church. With verse 11 Paul completes the circle of his total argument in 9:33–10:13 by once again quoting the very passage with which he began— Isaiah 28:16. This Rabbinic style of argument shows the earnestness with which Paul seeks to convince his Jewish brethren of the need to bow in humble gratitude to God for the true stone in Zion.

"For there is no distinction between Jew and Greek, the same Lord is Lord of all and bestows his riches upon all who call upon him" (10:12). This summary sentence tells of the end of one era and the beginning of the new.

Line (A) discovers its fulfillment in Christ. The nature

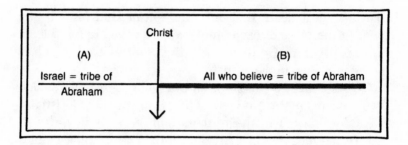

of that fulfillment is so total, so radically complete that following Christ's word and work a whole New Israel (line B)
becomes the continuation of the holy history. Put another
way, what Paul is teaching in 10:12 is that Israel discovers
in its completion (the coming of Christ) that the Lord of
Israel is Lord of all. Because of the wideness of his reign
all who answer his grace with their own "Yea" are granted
the riches of his grace.

Paul closes the thesis with a final Old Testament prophetic
quotation, in this case from Joel 2:32, the very quotation that
was so pivotal in Peter's sermon (Acts 2).

In this next passage (10:14–21) the Apostle raises a series
of questions which are then answered by a collection of Old
Testament references: Isaiah 52:7 in verse 15; Isaiah 53:1 in
verse 20; Isaiah 65:2 in verse 21.

The series of questions on Paul's comment in verse 17—
"So faith comes from what is heard, and what is heard comes
by the preaching of Christ"—fit together to form two main
propositions. The first is that all men, Jews and Greeks alike,
must hear the announcement concerning Christ in order to
reply to that word. Without this hearing event happening
then faith is impossible, because faith involves the human
choice, the human response.

Paul's second proposition is that the Gentiles, who lacked
the long tradition of relationship with the Law and Prophets,
are now by their faith in Christ fulfilling a wondrous part of
Old Testament prophecy (Deut. 32:21; Isa. 65:1), which

foresaw the immensity of the hope in Christ. The irony of the phenomenon of Gentile faith is that it is not matched by faith from among all of Israel. But Paul points out that even this disobedience in Israel is foretold in Isaiah 65:2.

As chapter 10 closes, Paul has explained by the preceding arguments the greatness of the fulfillment of Israel and the tragedy of the discontinuity of Israel in disobedience.

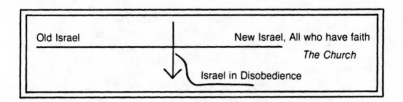

Old Israel | New Israel, All who have faith | *The Church* | Israel in Disobedience

Section 5—11:1–36—THE MYSTERY OF GRACE

11: 1)I ask, then, has God rejected his people? By no means! I myself am an Israelite, a descendant of Abraham, a member of the tribe of Benjamin. 2)God has not rejected his people whom he foreknew. Do you not know what the scripture says of Elijah, how he pleads with God against Israel? 3)"Lord, they have killed thy prophets, they have demolished thy altars, and I alone am left, and they seek my life." 4)But what is God's reply to him? "I have kept for myself seven thousand men who have not bowed the knee to Baal." 5)So too at the present time there is a remnant, chosen by grace.

6)But if it is by grace, it is no longer on the basis of works; otherwise grace would no longer be grace. 7) What then? Israel failed to obtain what it sought. The elect obtained it, but the rest were hardened, 8)as it is written, "God gave them a spirit of stupor, eyes that should not see and ears that should not hear, down to this very day." 9)And David says, "Let their feast become a snare and a trap, a pitfall and a retribution for them; 10)let their eyes be darkened so that they cannot see, and bend their backs for ever."

11)So I ask, have they stumbled so as to fall? By no means! But through their trespass salvation has come to the Gentiles, so as to make Israel jealous. 12)Now if their trespass means riches for the world, and if their failure means riches for the Gentiles. how much more will their full inclusion mean! 13)Now I am speaking to you Gentiles. Inasmuch then as I am an apostle to the Gentiles, I magnify my ministry 14)in order to make my fellow Jews jealous, and thus save some of them. 15)For if their rejection means the reconciliation of the world, what will their acceptance mean but life from the dead? 16)If the dough offered as first fruits is holy, so is the whole lump; and if the root is holy, so are the branches. 17)But if some of the branches were broken off, and you, a wild olive shoot, were grafted in their place to share the richness of the olive tree, 18)do not boast over the branches. If you do boast, remember it is not you that support the root, but the root that supports you. 19)You will say, "Branches were broken off so that I might be grafted in." 20)That is true. They were broken off because of their unbelief, but you stand fast only through faith. So do not become proud, but stand in awe. 21)For if God did not spare the natural branches, neither will he spare you.

22)Note then the kindness and the severity of God: severity toward those who have fallen, but God's kindness to you, provided you continue in his kindness; otherwise you too will be cut off. 23)And even the others, if they do not persist in their unbelief, will be grafted in, for God has the power to graft them in again. 24)For if you have been cut from what is by nature a wild olive tree. and grafted, contrary to nature, into a cultivated olive tree, how much more will these natural branches be grafted back into their own olive tree. 25)Lest you be wise in your own conceits, I want you to understand this mystery, brethren: a hardening has come upon part of Israel, until the full number of the Gentiles come in, 26) and so all Israel will be saved; as it is written, "The Deliverer will come from Zion, he will banish ungodliness from Jacob"; 27)and this will be my covenant with them when I take away their sins."

28)As regards the gospel they are enemies of God, for your sake; but as regards election they are beloved for the sake of their forefathers. 29)For the gifts and the call of God are irrevocable. 30)Just as you were once disobedient to God but now have received mercy because of their disobedience, 31)so they have now been disobedient in order that by the mercy shown to you they also may receive mercy. 32)For God has consigned all men to disobedience, that he may have mercy upon all. 33)O the depth of the riches and wisdom and knowledge of God! How unsearchable are his judgments and how inscrutable his ways! 34)"For who has known the mind of the Lord, or who has been his counselor?" 35)"Or who has given a gift to him that he might be repaid?" 36)For from him and through him and to him are all things. To him be glory for ever. Amen.

"I ask, then, has God rejected his people?" (11:1). The Apostle first of all makes it clear that there are members of Israel's race who are indeed a part of that new Israel line.

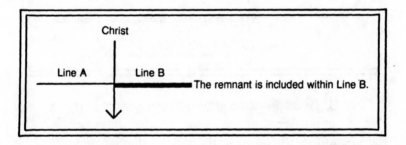

He refers to the remnant theology of the Old Testament to explain that this too was foretold (see verse 3 in which he quotes the incident in Elijah's life, 1 Kings 19). This teaching militates against the possible idea that Israel had in fact been canceled out and destroyed by Christ. The right word to use is "complete"—*telos*. There is now the remnant, as there always has been in the history of Abraham's people, who have trusted in God's grace. Paul carefully heads off any "Galatian" problem in verse 6. "But if it is grace, it is no longer on the basis of works; otherwise grace would no longer be grace." The one new line contains Jew and Greek, together and by God's grace one. The Jew is not superior to the Greek since both are debtors to the love of God. The Greek is not superior to the Jew since both are debtors to the love of God.

Israel in discontinuity lives under the judgment of God.

The Apostle quotes Isaiah 29:10 and Deuteronomy 29:4 in an interpretive quotation that combines parts of each (8). Finally, the harsh words of the Psalmist in Psalm 69:22 ff. are paraphrased and interpreted as applicable to Israel itself when it rejects its true king. The picture is grim, and unless God himself acts there can be no hope for Israel in discontinuity (11:11–36).

11:11 "So I ask, have they stumbled so as to fall?"

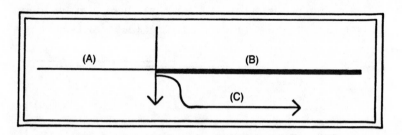

Line C, Israel in disobedience, now occupies the Apostle's attention. What are the prospects for these people? At the opening of sections 9, 10, and 11, Paul had said concerning their tragedy, "I have great sorrow and unceasing anguish in my heart" (9:2). This opening statement made clear his view of the gravity of the crisis of Israel in discontinuity. Now Paul faces the question, What is its final destiny? To "fall?" The reality of the stumbling has been carefully explained by Paul in chapters 9 and 10; now he must face up to the outcome of the discontinuity.

"By no means" (11:11). The apparently relentless logic of the separated drift of Israel in disobedience is interrupted.

Paul will now bring into focus one more proposition with two parts:

God is not finished with Israel even though Israel is rebellious. This is the thesis of the remaining verses of Romans 11. There are two lines of thought that establish this thesis. The first line of reasoning is found in 11:11, "But through their trespass salvation has come to the Gen-

tiles, *so as to make Israel jealous.*" Paul's point is that the
rebel Israel, when given time, will repent and desire inclusion in the new Israel. This for Paul is an existential argument supported by his own life story. It is in this context
that he warns the Gentiles against anti-Semitism, that is,
feelings of resentment or fear toward the unbelieving part of
Israel. The Apostle indirectly urges his Gentile Christian
friends to live their Christian lives in such a way that their
love will make the nonbelievers eager to unite with the
new Israel and seek Christ. He also reminds the reader that
God is the only one able to graft in the branches. By the
same logic God is ultimately the only one who is the judge
of all, both Jew and Gentile (11:17-24). "By raising the
matter of this regrafting, Paul demonstrates a definite pro-
gression in his thought. Unmistakably this is an open door:
over against all talk of irrevocability and closed situations,
Paul refers to God's 'power to graft them in again.' "[5]

"I want you to understand this mystery" (11:25). With
these words Paul introduces the second line of reasoning.
There are several critical questions that interpreters have
struggled with in this complex section (11:25-36). The two
most pressing have to do with the *time* frame of the passage, and secondly with the actual identification of what
Paul means by the term *Israel* in verse 26, "And so all Israel
will be saved." John Calvin interpreted "all Israel" as referring to the church: Israel and Gentiles together, "all people
of God." In the terms of our diagram for these chapters,
Calvin feels verse 26 refers to Line B, now including those

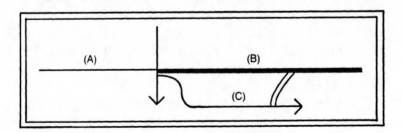

from Line C who have repented as described by Paul in
11:11–24. But such an interpretation is not exegetically fair
to the customary use of the word "Israel" by Paul in the
context of Romans 9, 10, and 11.

An even more complex exegetical issue for interpretation
concerns the time frame for the phrase "*until* the full number . . . and so all Israel *will* be saved . . ." (11:25, 26).
Dr. Berkouwer agrees that it is hazardous for interpreters
to over-read the time references in terms of the previously
ordered eschatological expectations of the reader. "Paul was
not preoccupied with Israel's distant future, but with what
he could see . . . when he sees the mercy shown to the
Gentiles, his eyes turn once again to Israel. He does not
think in chronological categories, nor does he speculate
about hidden mysteries. . . . He is simply concerned with
the Israel of his day . . ."[6]

I appreciate the concern of Dr. Berkouwer to preserve the
pastoral nature of these sentences in Paul. However, there is
no escaping Paul's own dramatic setting for the mystery that
he is privileged to share with the church. God is not finished
with Israel even though his people are rebellious. He will
win them to faith. The reality of the historically new Israel
—Jews and Greeks together in the forever family of God—
will make them jealous and eager to repent and find life.

In this context the Apostle expounds the mystery that God
will be far more successful in this mission than the new Israel
Christians (Line B) may presently expect. I believe that
this is the contextual setting of Paul's subsequent sentences
(11:25–32). Within that setting Paul tells of the mystery of
eventual salvation of "all Israel." He gives no clues as to how
this victory over unbelief is to be won, nor does he tech-
nically define "all Israel" (11:26, 32). Paul leaves the reader
breathless with the sweeping language: *All Israel* (11:26)
all to disobedience . . . mercy upon *all* (11:32).

God is able to win men and women from unbelief to faith,
to win them to Jesus Christ. Paul shares his unshakable con-

fidence in the immensity of the gospel's appeal and wonder. "It has been objected that Paul here lets his patriotism override his logic. He has emphasized more than once in the Epistle that natural descent from the patriarchs is not what matters in God's sight. . . . It might suffice to say 'the heart has its reasons that reason cannot know' (Pascal) but there is more than that to be said. Paul has a deeper and clearer insight into God's grace than his critics; if God's grace operated in accordance with strict logic, the outlook would be dismal for Jews and Gentiles alike."[7]

Here then, in the final part of these chapters, the third and fourth of the striking paradoxes are portrayed.

On the one side the discontinuity of Israel in disobedience is taught as an actual reality. On the other side, Paul teaches that in spite of this fact God is not caught without moves that he may take.

The most critical of all the paradoxes is posed in 11:25–26.

On the one side there is no escape from freedom. Men and women have the right and obligation to reply to God's grace. This is faith, and Paul teaches it on every side. "Every one who has faith may be justified" (10:4). "So faith comes from what is heard, and what is heard comes by the preaching of Christ" (10:17).

Now alongside the reality of the freedom of man and the call by God to turn and believe in order to be saved, Paul insists upon the mystery of the freedom of God. For this reason he begins the passage 11:25 with a warning to the Christian not to confine the Lord. What God may or may not do belongs to his own counsel. This is the doctrine of election in its most generic form.

In my judgment, both theologically and devotionally, the Christian must keep the paradoxes of Romans 9, 10, and 11 intact as they are also kept intact by Paul.

The stance of the Apostle is one of awe as he concludes the passage with quotations from Isaiah 40 and Job 35:7. The resolution to these paradoxes that Paul offers is the resolution of Job himself after he hears Elihu and the Lord speak to him, "I know that thou canst do all things, and that no purpose of thine can be thwarted" (Job 42:2).

"Here is the possibility of God pressing upon us, vastly nigh at hand, vastly rich, but also vastly beyond our understanding."[8]

A Review

The Book of Romans began with a crisis. The Apostle led his readers through a stormy courtroom scene in 1:18–3:20 in which the stern appraisal of mankind in those opening sentences of the book made its uncompromised mark. Paul established the source of the crisis—the problem of broken relationship—and he pointed up the cumulative nature of crisis.

The love of God was alive and real even in the rebuke of Romans 1–3, just as it is Sonia who as the one who really loves Raskolnikov in Dostoyevsky's *Crime and Punishment,* is the one who cries out to Raskolnikov, "You are a murderer." God's love creates more guilt in man than the pointed fingers of a dozen courtroom prosecutors. This love, with freedom and justice in it, is at the core of the prosecution words of Romans 1–3. But it is a dangerous thing to stir up within the human personality the awareness of its own alienation and guilt as Paul dares to do in Romans 1–3. He unmasks the idolatry of man for what it is—immoral and self-destructive. He challenges the pretensions of religious man. He portrays the human crisis in the language of Old Testament judgment passages, "None is righteous, no, not one . . . their feet are swift to shed blood . . . the way of peace they do not know . . ." (3:10).

But the Sonia who accuses Raskolnikov and urges him to surrender to the police is the one who follows him to prison in Siberia. Love as great as this is not afraid of real guilt because it is able to heal the one who is broken by sin. "In

Jesus Christ we have discovered that the grace of God and the omnipotence of God are the same thing" (Karl Barth). It is Paul's confidence in the power of the love of God to heal every brokenness in man that forms the foundation of the opening prosecution section as well as the whole of the Book of Romans.

Romans 3:21–5:21 is the story of cumulative grace. The love of God is not a static, fixed point, like the sterile pronouncement of innocent or guilty within a courtroom. Justification means the dynamic reconciliation of broken relationships. In Romans 6, 7, and 8, Paul shares his definition of a Christian as seen in the context of the tension between the claim of grace and the weakness of men. Romans 9, 10, and 11 contains Paul's interpretation of Israel in the context of the freedom of God and the freedom of man.

Now in Part 7 of our study we will see Paul build upon the foundation of chapters 1–11 to develop a strategy for the survival of the Christian in an age of stress and peril. But Paul has more in mind than survival alone. He presents in these chapters a strategy for mission by the Christians within the real world. This missional strategy was first introduced in 8:28–39. Now following the historical overview of chapters 9, 10, and 11, the Apostle turns his attention toward the meaning of the Christian and the community of Christians in the world.

Part 7

Strategy for Survival
of the Church

Section 1—Romans 12:1-2—BELIEVE GOD

> 12: 1)I appeal to you therefore, brethren, by the mer-
> cies of God, to present your bodies as a living sacrifice,
> holy and acceptable to God, which is your spiritual
> worship. 2)Do not be conformed to this world but be
> transformed by the renewal of your mind, that you
> may prove what is the will of God, what is good and
> acceptable and perfect.

"I appeal to you . . . to present . . ." Paul begins chapter 12 with the critical moment—the freedom of faith. The
verb "present" (*paristēmi*) was earlier used and translated
in that text by the RSV with the word "yield." The word is
by connotation more concrete than cerebral. It becomes an
essential part of Paul's faith vocabulary.

In view of the grace of God, in the light of God's love, the
Apostle now calls upon his readers to believe. Two recent
translations have caught the force of the connection of grace
and faith in the sentence.

> "Think of God's mercy, my brothers, and worship
> him, I beg you, in a way that is worthy . . . by

offering of our living bodies" (Jerusalem Bible).
"Therefore, my brothers, I implore you by God's
mercy to offer yourselves to him" (NEB).

The source of a concrete act of belief is the concrete event
of God's decision in man's behalf.

"It is not the case that Paul turns to exhortation when he
cannot sustain his declarations. Quite the reverse, the im-
perative is spoken because the indicative is true."[1]

Paul summarizes the portrayal of chapters 1–11 with the
word (*oiktirmōn*) "mercies," a word that emphasizes the
particular acts of love by God. The exhortation that calls
men to have faith originates from the objective fact of God's
love. Because of the truth of the self-disclosure of God's love,
we are encouraged by the Apostle to make our own move of
self-disclosure.

Let us examine the meaning of faith as Paul draws together the faith threads of the whole book into the dramatic
sentences of Romans 12:1–6. In the perspective of these
verses, let us ask, "What is *faith* for the Apostle Paul?"

(1) Faith is the human response to God's prior acts. This
means that faith is relative and not absolute. It is the love
of God that triggers human faith and not faith which creates
the love of God. Man's faith does not control or administer
the grace of God as Paul has clearly shown in Romans 3:21–
31 and 11:29. This means that it is faith that is the relative
fact and grace that is the absolute fact. Only God is absolute. Therefore, faith can never be absolute; it is always a
growing, dynamic reality—with ups and downs. Paul's choice
of the word "body" (*soma*) is intended to thwart all attempts to exalt human faith. But in fact on many divergent
fronts faith is often glorified. We see this glorification of
faith in some forms of pietism where the acts and experiences of faith tend to overshadow the objective source of
ιaith. The exaltation of faith is also the one most important
clue to the interpretation of the theology of Rudolph Bult-

mann. Bultmann rightly understands the vital significance of man's faith choice, and I fully agree with his statement.

> Before God man stands . . . in utter loneliness . . . the fundamental question which is asked of man, "Are you ready to believe in the Word of God's grace?" can only be answered individually.[2]

Faith in the Old and New Testaments is man's individual answer to God's grace. In the setting of Romans 12:1-2 it cannot be otherwise. A person can only give his own body. But that faith soon takes over everything else in the theology of Professor Bultmann. For him, the Easter faith of the early church becomes the real absolute, and the facts upon which faith is founded become the relative ingredients that are arranged, weighed, and in the end, even possibly created by the *faith* of the Christians. Ernst Käsemann challenges his teacher on this issue.

> Bultmann expressly adopts as his own H. Braun's statement "The constant is the self-understanding of the believer; christology is the variable." I hold this judgment to be, quite simply, false and to pick up Bultmann's own distinction, false both historically and materially.[3]

The fact is that for Paul, and the other New Testament writers, faith is not glorified to such an extent as this. Faith is the response of men to the prior act of God. The freedom of faith in the New Testament church does not boldly create accounts of the life of Jesus to help make the gospel of God more meaningful to the real people in the first century. New Testament faith is not ultimate in itself. Faith is the act of men and women which receive that which is the true ultimate—the grace of God revealed in Jesus Christ. Therefore, Christian faith is able to accept human complexity and incompleteness. For this reason also it grows. For this reason it can survive doubt.

(2) This brings us to a second observation about faith as the Apostle Paul presents it. For Paul, faith is *the concrete response of the whole person.* Dr. Barth comments on Paul's use of the word *soma.* "Now the body is the observable, historical man, of whom alone we have knowledge . . . This rules out an obedience affecting only the 'inner' life of the soul or the mind."[4]

As we observed in Part 6, the Apostle is thinking in whole terms when he speaks of faith. The Christian is called to present his whole self to Christ. That is, problematic me, the self I know—with fears, doubts, hopes, and trust intermingled and even turbulently so. Now we can understand why grace must be prior to faith. If faith in God means the bringing of the whole self to the Lord and not simply the religious or spiritual inner flame, then it would not be possible unless God himself were to take the initiative toward us. Only his love gives to us the courage that dares to present our real selves, what we really are, to him. As the love of God has been disclosed within the concreteness of real history—"he suffered under Pontius Pilate," "Christ died for us" (Rom. 5:8)—so in the same way Paul challenges his readers to be concrete, "present your bodies a living sacrifice. . . . This is your ritual." Men are religious and want to do something religious. The curious phrase "which is your spiritual worship" could be translated *the liturgical ritual.* Paul is saying in effect, "Present your real selves to Christ, the living sacrifice; this is all the ritual you need." The gospel of redemption of chapters 1–11 is also vitally present in the sentence. As persons in response to God's grace present their real selves, they are then assured that such an act of faith is "holy and acceptable to God." Paul is not calling upon the Christian first to become holy in order to have an adequate faith. He is saying that the result of our trust in God's salvation is that he grants holiness and acceptance.

(3) *Faith is freedom,* the freedom to move, to act, and be. Here in Romans 12–16 the Apostle will describe a game

plan for the Christian in the world, a strategy which calls for thoughtful, creative moves on the part of the Christians. Freedom is the correct and accurate word to characterize the style of life that now occupies the final pages of the Book of Romans. Paul has spoken of freedom earlier in the book. In these final chapters, the portrayal of chapters 6, 7, and 8 will be historically stated in terms of actual situations in which every one of the Christians at Rome must live his life.

The freedom thesis is instituted by a challenge, "Be not conformed to this age, but be transformed by the renewal of your mind. . . ." The word *schēma* is translated "conformed"—"squeezed" by J. B. Phillips. "Transformed" is the RSV translation of the word *meta morphē*. Aristotle is the first in Greek literature to decisively set the meaning of *morphē*. "In Aristotle true (idea) and (*morphē*) are identical. *Morphē* equals the form which is the aggregate of the qualities of a thing. The difference between *morphē* and *schēma* is tested by the fact that the *morphē*, or a definite thing as such, for instance of a lion or a tree, is the only, while its *schēma* may change every minute."[5] Lightfoot points out that in the New Testament *schēma* retains the sense of changeableness (as in 1 Cor. 7:31, 2 Pet. 1:14, 2 Cor. 11:13, 14, 15), whereas *morphē* connotes the essential and whole nature (as noted in the usages of Rom. 8:29, Phil. 3:10, 2 Cor. 3:18, Gal. 4:19).

How then do we understand Paul's sentence "Do not be conformed to this world"? These words amount to a dare to the Christian to challenge the right of the present age (era) to schematize the one who trusts in God—that is, to impress its shape upon the Christian's life. The theological premise for Paul's exhortation is this: The Christian does not receive the definition of who he is or the valuation of what he is worth from the created order but from the Creator. It is God's decision that gives meaning both to the whole and to the parts. This is the teaching of Romans 8:31–39.

Therefore, Paul's statement asks by implication the question, By what authority does one part of the whole, which itself is mortal and penultimate, have the right to conform and distort to its own design another part of that whole? Yet, this very experience of exploitation, coercion and definition is common to all men. *Schēmata* is a word that twentieth-century man knows very well by his own programmed experiences. Paul means by that word the captivity of idols (1:18–23), the brutalization of man that occurs when he is programmed, defined, and ascribed meaning on the basis of what is not God.

The world age (*aeon*) in this passage refers to the whole of the transient age. By this is included the forces within this mortal age: man himself, spiritual forces, demons, the devil, angels. (See also Paul's use of this term in 2 Cor. 1:20, 2:6, 3:18.) In the theology of the Old and New Testaments, all of these belong to the created order. Heaven and earth, each shall pass away. Only God himself, Father, Son, Holy Spirit, is eternal. Only God himself grants the meaning that deserves to shape human life. Therefore, Paul urges the Christians at Rome to precipitate a crisis against such *schēmata* shapings of man himself by what is not God. There is similarity in this passage with the exhortations of Romans 6:12–14 and Colossians 2:8–3:17. The Colossian text stands as an enlargement or commentary on the one line challenge of Romans 12:1–2: ". . . but be transformed by the renewal of your mind, that you may prove what is the will of God, what is good and acceptable and perfect."

Let us now examine Paul's solution to the stresses put upon man and his integrity by the age in which he exists.

Morphē, "the aggregate of the qualities of a thing." The change of the whole, aggregate person by God's creative work—this is Paul's strategy for survival in the face of the outward pressures of *schēma*. Paul offers no escape from the pressures of the age, and his nonescapist intention is preserved in these verses by such words as *soma* (body), and *meta morphē* (transformation of the whole self). For Paul, the renewal of the mind results in the Christian's grasping the will of God for his life here and now as a disciple (living sacrifice) of the Lord. He discovers that God's will is good (*agathon*—the word means "kind"), acceptable (*evareston* —the word used earlier in 12:1), and (*teleion*—the word in 10:4 which means "complete").

Paul is saying that there is a way to endure the *schēmata* of the Roman world. That way is made possible for the Christian, the aggregate whole person, as he is changed by the grace of God under the very noses of the programmers. It is the *Way of Freedom,* and the remainder of Romans will explain this new way.

Section 2—Romans 12:3–21—HOPE

12: 3)For by the grace given to me I bid every one among you not to think of himself more highly than he ought to think, but to think with sober judgment, each according to the measure of faith which God has assigned him. 4)For as in one body we have many members, and all the members do not have the same function, 5)so we, though many, are one body in Christ, and individually members one of another. 6) Having gifts that differ according to the grace given to us, let us use them: if prophecy, in proportion to our faith; if service, in our serving; he who teaches, in his teaching; 8)he who exhorts, in his exhortation; he who contributes, in liberality; he who gives aid, with zeal; he who does acts of mercy, with cheerfulness.

9)Let love be genuine; hate what is evil, hold fast to what is good; 10) love one another with brotherly affection; outdo one another in showing honor. 11) Never flag in zeal, be aglow with the Spirit, serve the Lord. 12)Rejoice in your hope, be patient in tribulation, be constant in prayer. 13)Contribute to the needs of the saints, practice hospitality. 14)Bless those who persecute you; bless and do not curse them. 15) Rejoice with those who rejoice, weep with those who weep. 16)Live in harmony with one another; do not be haughty, but associate with the lowly; never be conceited. 17)Repay no one evil for evil, but take thought

for what is noble in the sight of all. 18)If possible, so
far as it depends upon you, live peaceably with all.
19)Beloved, never avenge yourselves, but leave it to
the wrath of God; for it is written, "Vengeance is mine,
I will repay, says the Lord." 20)No, "if your enemy is
hungry, feed him; if he is thirsty, give him drink; for
by so doing you will heap burning coals upon his
head." 21)Do not be overcome by evil, but overcome
evil with good.

The Jerusalem Bible translates verse 3 as follows, "In the
light of the grace I have received I want to urge each one
among you not to exaggerate his real importance."

The sentence begins as if it were a review of the portrait
of the Christian in chapters 6, 7, and 8. Paul calls upon the
Christian disciple, now embarked on the way to freedom, to
remember his own humanity—to think of himself soberly
and without exaggeration. This same thesis also appears in
1 Corinthians 12:14–26 (see also Phil. 2:1–4). What is remarkable in this sentence (12:3) is Paul's decisive use of the
two words "grace" and "faith." Their use imparts to his
counsel the implications of real significance for the doctrine
of sanctification. Paul teaches in this verse that because of
the grace of God the Christian person is set free from exaggeration. It is only grace that enables the Christian to look
realistically at who he is because of the fact that his salvation
and sanctification do not depend upon an idealistic self-
assessment. Quite the opposite, grace means that God's love
has overcome every pretense. All pretension is swept away
at the cross when the Christian first becomes a disciple of
Jesus. So now in the journey of discipleship, the grace of
God continues to sweep aside everything unreal. Christ alone
is able to forgive sin, and he alone is able to sustain that forgiveness. Therefore, Paul's counsel to realism is founded
upon the reality of *grace*.

Faith is also decisive within Paul's sentence. His thesis is
that the Christian's growth in the freedom of faith is itself
the gift of God, "the measure of faith which God has as-

signed him." Now we can better understand Calvin's source
for his statement, "Freedom is not so much man's free choice
but man set free by God." Faith is human freedom in its
highest form; it is real because God makes it real.

Paul teaches that the more faith the Christian has, the
more he is able to accept who he is in the light of God's
grace. In other words, faith means that the Christian sees
himself in a mediated way; Christ has interposed his grace
into the matrix of the Christian's self-understanding. Therefore Paul is able to counsel modesty. Because of faith there
is no need to play games with God, with others, or with the
self; the one thing that faith is not is self-deception, illusion.
It is important to observe that this sentence comes just before the Apostle's teaching concerning gifts and the church.
This means that the realism brought by grace and faith to
the Christian's relationship with God and with himself is
also essential for his relationships with the community of
faith. Paul warns against doctrines of sanctification which
encourage exaggeration. This sentence is another example
of the reality orientation of the gospel.

"One body in Christ many members" (12:4–5). This sentence is almost identical to the sentence in 1 Corinthians
12:12. The interpreter may rightly consider the long discussion of Paul in 1 Corinthians 12, 13, and 14 as the Apostle's commentary upon the more briefly stated formula in
Romans 12:4–8.

Paul makes use of the model or image of the body to teach
the Romans the inescapable relationship to their fellow
Christians. The relational model that we first encountered
in the Apostle's prosecution section (1:18–3:20) to show the
crisis of man is now presented in its fulfillment to teach the
meaning of the Christian's life in the world. As in our crisis
we could not escape the neighbor, so now in the joy of God's
grace we are brought into relationship with our brothers and
sisters.

The brokenness represented by the intersecting lines has

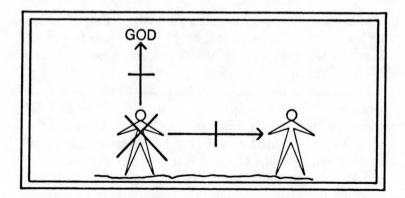

been resolved by God's own act in man's behalf. It is Jesus Christ who has come alongside as the mediator. He has taken upon himself the brokenness of man's selfhood. He has taken upon himself the sin of man expressed horizontally, vertically, and internally. Christ the mediator has resolved the human tragedy not from the distance of eternity but within time, within history itself.

The Christian is the one who has said yes to the mediator as Savior and Lord (5:1, 12:1–2). Becoming a Christian means discipleship of the individual Christian in obedience to the Lord Jesus Christ (1:5). The uniqueness of the claim upon the individual is essential. In the context of Romans 12 we can only present our own body—not that of the tribe or of someone else. But Paul now teaches in detail what has been inferred in chapters 9, 10, and 11, that faith in Jesus Christ results in a dramatic new relationship for the be-

liever. Christ the mediator brings the Christian into reconciled friendship not only with God but also with every
other individual who answers yes to the mediator. This new
relationship of faith is the church. To be in Christ grants to
the believer the inescapable body relationship with every
other person who by faith is also in Christ (1:7). This community, the body of Christ, is to predominate Paul's concern
in the final four chapters of the Book of Romans.

In Christ. What does Paul mean by this phrase which appears so often in his letters (Eph. 1:1; Col. 2:6; Phil. 2:1)?
The context in Romans 12:5 is relational. We are a whole
people in Christ; as unique individuals we are related to him,
and because of him to each other. Paul's thesis is this: The
relationship with Christ liberates the Christian to be related
to the body of Christ. The "in Christ" phrase is the theological description of Paul's doctrine of the ministry of the
Holy Spirit. (In this connection, note especially the language
of 8:1, and 9.) The Holy Spirit assures the Christian of his
secure place in the love of Christ, not as an observer of that
love but as a participant. This means that the phrase "in
Christ" is a pastoral statement to the believer that indeed
God has heard the yes of human faith.

"Having gifts that differ according to the grace given to
us" (12:6-8). The Apostle in this passage allots only a very
brief discussion to the matter of gifts, whereas in the Corinthian letter the development is more complete and extensive.
He reminds the Romans that by the grace of God gifts are
granted to the members of the body. *Charismata* is the word
translated "gifts" in the English text. *Charis* which is the
root of *charismata* is the word "grace." The emphasis of the
text is threefold.

(1) The gifts are given by the decision of God to the individual Christian and for the whole body of Christians.
The brief list of gifts that Paul includes in this passage supports the teaching in Corinthians and Ephesians that the
gifts given to individual Christians are intended to benefit

the whole community in its mission and faith. "To each is given the manifestation of the Spirit for the common good" (1 Cor. 12:7). "And his gifts were that some should be apostles, some prophets, some evangelists, some pastors and teachers, for the equipment of the saints for the work of ministry" (Eph. 4:11, 12).

(2) Paul teaches that the gifts are unique and differ from person to person. This fact of diversity in gifts is proof of the richness of the Christian life. Paul's argument in 1 Corinthians 12, 13, and 14 is that the gifts belong to the body and not the body to the gifts. The meaning of the single member of the body depends upon his relationship to the Lord of the body and not upon his gift. This is the critical importance for Paul of his use of the phrase *in Christ*. The church does not confer meaning to the Christian. "The eye cannot say to the hand, I have no need of thee." The individual Christian does not by his own self-awareness or spiritual mood of the moment determine his true meaning. "Because I am not an eye, I do not belong to the body." The missionary task and the gift that accompanies it do not determine the meaning of the Christians.

Charismata is an implication of *charis*. This means that grace is what is prior. Meaning for the Christian and for Christendom is dependent upon Christ. The Apostle's argument is fundamental and obvious. Nevertheless the gifted Christian community at Corinth succeeded in reversing the order. Perhaps the Apostle's experience with this Corinthian reversal influenced the logical order of this paragraph (12:3–8). Before Paul mentions the gifts and the gifted, he establishes the level ground, "By grace . . . I bid every one of you not to think of himself more highly than he ought to think."

(3) Freedom is the third emphasis present in the Apostle Paul's teaching concerning gifts, "Having gifts that differ . . . let us use them" (12:6). The freedom of the Christian taught in a bold and even negative sense in 12:2—"Challenge the idols of this age"—is now taught in the context of

the Christian's positive task in the world. Paul's warning against exaggeration in verse 3 does not immobilize the creativity and freedom of the Christian to get on with the job. Making use of the gifts that God has provided, developing his or her stride as a Christian person within the church—this is Christian obligation and freedom. Here freedom is understood not only as freedom *from* bondage but freedom *to* and *toward* meaning and responsibility.

"Let love be genuine. . . ." (12:9–21). This beautiful passage consists of the Apostle's counsel to the Christians at Rome concerning the marks of a Christian style of life in the midst of the real world. It becomes very clear in this passage that Paul envisages neither individual nor communal escape from the present age. Words like "tribulation," "persecute" (literally in Greek "those who hunt down"), "weep," "evil," "enemy," make it clear that Paul believes that it is possible to survive as a Christian in the less than ideal setting of the first century. More than that, Paul is teaching a strategy for victory in the contest. He foresees a victory in that the Christian is free to break the ancient reciprocal cycle of enmity and hurtfulness between people. "Bless those who persecute you. . . ." Paul believes that "enemy" is a relative, not an absolute word; therefore, he calls for a strategy of love in the face of alienation.

It is within this paragraph that Paul presents the image of "coals of fire."

> These "coals" distress his spirit . . . this is the only way to achieve a true conversion; namely, through love and kindness. For he who is converted through threats and terror is never truly converted as long as he retains that form of conversion. For fear makes him hate his conversion. . . .[6]

"Do not be overcome by evil, but overcome evil with good" (12:21). The theological source for this optimistic final sentence of the Apostle is found within the text as a

whole in verse 12, "Rejoice in your hope." It is precisely
Paul's hope that energizes his ethics. In fact, a careful reading of this passage (12:9–21) reveals that the counsel will
not really make sense apart from the conviction that Jesus
Christ is the reigning Lord and that history's future is in his
hands. For this reason Paul is able to reject the law of the
jungle—reciprocity, evil for evil—in favor of the revolutionary and new law, "overcome evil with good." Literally,
in the good. For this reason, because of hope, Paul possesses
an authentic strategy as far as man and his society are concerned. Paul dares to believe that persecutors can be won
over and made whole. This is Paul's strategy—he dares to
trust in the victory won by Jesus Christ.

> This radical openness for the future is the Chris-
> tian's freedom. . . . The stoic is free because of
> his reason. He concentrates on reason by turning
> his back on all encounters and claims from the out-
> side world. This makes him free from the future.
> . . . Paul, on the other hand, is free because he
> has been made free by the grace of God. . . . He
> becomes free for the future. . . . The stoic shuts
> the door to all encounters and lives in the timeless
> logic. The Christian opens himself to these en-
> counters, and lives from the future.[7]

In Paul's view of history, Jesus Christ stands at the end
of history, just as surely as he stands at the decisive center
and beginning. Paul looks in hope to the fulfillment of history in Jesus Christ, and therefore the love present in his
ethics (as we see in 12:9–21) is motivated not only by the
event in the past—the cross of Jesus—but also by the reign
of that same Jesus Christ in the present and in the future.
  This confidence in the meaningful goal of history founded
in the victory of Jesus Christ is the source of Christian ethics;
more than that it is also the compelling urgency of ethics in
the Christian sense. The love of God—past, present, future

—is both the cause of Paul's rejoicing and the reason for his urgency (2 Cor. 5:13–21).

> Grace means divine impatience . . . grace is the enemy of the most indispensable "interim ethic," grace is the axe laid to the root of the good conscience which we modern men always wish to enjoy . . . in point of fact it is grace alone that is competent to provide men with a truly ethical disturbance. . . .[8]

Section 3—Preface

The Apostle Paul's strategy for the survival and the mission of the Christian church is founded upon hope. Only the theology of hope makes sense of the exhortations of Paul in 12:9–21. He really believes that the love of Christ is stronger over the long course than the power of evil; for that reason he does not surrender to despair or panic. "The night is far gone. The day is at hand" (13:12). Paul shared with the apostolic church an expectation of the early return of Christ. What is remarkable about the letters of Paul is that this expectation does not result in sentimentalism or ethical insensitivity. But, as 12:9–21 demonstrates, the stance of the theology is realistic and ethically creative.

> It is not, therefore, correct as Overbeck and Albert Schweitzer maintain . . . to assert that the waiting for the end of the world in the apostolic age necessarily entailed the rejection of all culture . . . it should be noted that the faith in Christ, the Lord of the universe, which was theirs, contains a more positive germ of appreciation of first-century culture. . . .[9]

Chapter 13:1–7 illustrates Paul's understanding of the social order and its role in the daily life of societal man. I believe that Cullmann's observation can be established in many

places in the New Testament and in particular by the close
examination of these next seven verses.

Section 3—Romans 13:1-7

> 13: 1)Let every person be subject to the governing
> authorities. For there is no authority except from God,
> and those that exist have been instituted by God.
> 2)Therefore, he who resists the authorities resists what
> God has appointed, and those who resist will incur
> judgment. 3)For rulers are not a terror to good con-
> duct, but to bad. Would you have no fear of him who
> is in authority? Then do what is good, and you will
> receive his approval, 4)for he is God's servant for your
> good. But if you do wrong, be afraid, for he does not
> bear the sword in vain; he is the servant of God to
> execute his wrath on the wrongdoer. 5)Therefore, one
> must be subject, not only to avoid God's wrath but also
> for the sake of conscience. 6)For the same reason you
> also pay taxes, for the authorities are ministers of God,
> attending to this very thing. 7)Pay all of them their
> dues, taxes to whom taxes are due, revenue to whom
> revenue is due, respect to whom respect is due, honor
> to whom honor is due.

Paul, as political theorist, makes some major points in this
brief paragraph on the Christian citizen.

(1) Paul teaches that the social order which includes government with police authority is appointed by God as a
terror (phobe) to evil and an endorsement to good. This description realistically faces the possibility of crime in the
streets. Those who have read the first twelve chapters of
Romans are not taken by surprise at this portrait of the social order. It must of necessity recognize that mankind is
hostile to God, entrapped by idols, confused inwardly, is also
alienated in social relations. Therefore, persons and their
neighbors need the social arrangement or contract to protect
the one and the whole from exploitation. But Paul does not
limit his definition of the societal organization of the city to
its police function alone. He endorses its positive impor-

tance, too! The city, that is, man organized, is a force for good. Social contacts enable people to achieve social goals together that are impossible to achieve alone.

(2) The city is therefore good, but it is not ultimate! Before two sentences appear in this paragraph, Paul has both honored the social wholeness of man and at the same time he has limited its scale. ". . . Be subject to the governing authorities [dominion is the force of the Greek word]. For there is no authority [same word] except from God." The state has its task to perform, but its weight is measurable, limited, penultimate. The society of man, like the rest of the created order, is dependent upon the creator for its meaning. Think of the state as a series of real and necessary numbers, each with value yet within a parenthesis. In mathematics, all of the values of numbers and their relationships are decisively determined by the $+$ or $-$ sign that stands outside of the parentheses and which is prior to it.

$$+ \text{ or} - (8 + 9 - 7 - 8)$$

So it is with the state (Karl Barth).

(3) Paul's portrait of the social order is in ideal terms. We must not miss the significance of this ideal sketch of the social order. What the Apostle has done for man and his community is philosophically to insist that the ideal definition stand over against each of our particular experiences of the social whole. Put another way, Paul has presented in brief a confessional view of social order. The U.S. Constitution and Bill of Rights are also examples of a *confessional* criterion which then becomes for American society the check and balance (law and courts) over against both the people and their elected leaders. As in Paul's seven verses, the American document is an *ideal* statement of the meaning and goal of the social contract, a statement meant to exist in tension with the very society that brought it into being. That means that there are criteria by which the exercise of authority within the state is to be evaluated. The criteria presented in the paragraph 8:1–7 are threefold.

(a) That the social organization is not ultimate but rather is limited by the greater ultimacy of God himself.
(b) That the social organization is not a terror to good conduct.
(c) That the social organization is meant to be a deterrent to bad conduct.

The Apostle leaves the precise definition of the crucial variables in these three criteria to the reader. If it were Paul's intent to write a political instrument he would have been careful to state precisely the definitions, but this is not his goal.

(4) Paul is not concerned to construct a political schemata, because his intent in the paragraph is not so much theoretical as it is pastoral. He is concerned to keep his Christian brethren at Rome within the social whole and not out of it. Paul does not advocate withdrawal from the city of man with its streets and corners, some of which are dangerous. This paragraph demonstrates his concern for involvement with the social order. "You also pay taxes" and not only because of the authority of government, but because you want to be a part—"but also for the sake of conscience." The mission of the Christian community is to the very people who live in the city; therefore the Apostle could never encourage evasion of social ties that draw the people into orderly life together and the ties that preserve that order against chaos. We must remember that the Paul who writes these words is the Paul who knows the cities of the empire very well—the prisons, too.

Section 4—Romans 13:8–10—LOVE

13: 8)Owe no one anything, except to love one another; for he who loves his neighbor has fulfilled the law. 9)The commandments, "You shall not commit adultery, You shall not kill, You shall not steal, You shall not covet," and any other commandment, are summed up in this sentence, "You shall love your neighbor as yourself." 10)Love does no wrong to a neighbor; therefore, love is the fulfilling of the law.

Paul's teaching on the freedom of the Christian now reaches its ethical height. The Christian is set free by God's grace from the bondage of sin, the fear of death, and the power of the devil (8:31–39). Because of God's love, he is also set free from the unreality of super-spirituality and super-individualism (12:3–8). Within that paragraph (12:3–8) the Apostle encourages the Christians to discover and express their unique freedom gifts from God. "Having gifts that differ according to the grace given to us, *let us use them.*" Paul urges his Christian companions to put a strain upon the authenticity of their freedom from the captivity of this present age and its expectations by the love strategy of 12:14, "Bless those who persecute you." If the Christian is to follow that counsel, he will immediately discover that the way of freedom is as costly as it is powerful. Luther correctly assesses 12:9–21 as a test of freedom.

> Do not be overcome by evil but overcome evil with good. . . . See to it that he who hurts you does not cause you to become evil like him. . . . for he is the victor who changes another man to become like himself while he himself remains unchanged.[10]

To bless those who persecute is a test of the degree of freedom that the Christian knows.

Paul then places still another challenge before the way of freedom as he denounces the false freedom of anarchy in 13:1–7. Freedom does not "do its own thing" in isolation from the real street addresses and the rows of city houses of men and women in society. Paul very clearly preserves the freedom of discipleship in his exhortation: "One must be a good citizen, not only to avoid God's wrath, but also because he *wants* to . . ." (13:5). Now in the three verses of 13:8–10, Paul reaches the most crucial interpersonal test of the way of freedom that a Christian is to meet in his journey as a disciple of Christ. "Owe no one anything except to love one another . . ." (13:8). What we have in this sentence is a radical simplification of Christian ethics. The debt load in interpersonal encounter dominates all moral systems: the law of the jungle (fear—power); the law of the desert (proximity—distance—tribal relationship); the Law of Moses (boundaries, specific social commandments); laws in modern social organization (fear of reciprocity and penalty). Paul acknowledges in 13:1–7 the necessity of law in society, but he maintains that the Christian does not determine his relationship with other human beings by these systems; he acts toward the neighbor out of the freedom of love.

The question that we must consider now is this: What does the Apostle Paul mean by his use of the word love? "Except to love one another; for he who loves his neighbor has fulfilled the law." *Agapē* is the word Paul uses throughout the passage. In order to develop a definition of this word *agapē*, the student of the Greek language finds himself up against the curious problem that the word's meaning in classical (non-biblical) usage is so slight—there are very few uses of the word *agapē* in classical literature—that he must develop his definition from the uses of the word in the Septuagint and in the New Testament.[11] Within the limits of our commentary, what we desire is to observe Paul's use of *agapē* within Romans.

The word first appears in the greeting (1:7). "To all God's beloved in Rome." Here the word describes God's decision toward the Christians at Rome. They are loved by God.

The next usage is the introduction to the two Adams thesis (5:1–11) where *agapē* is contextually defined by the Apostle as follows, "Hope does not disappoint us, because God's love has been poured into our hearts through the Holy Spirit" (5:5). Love is here experienced within the Christian's life not only because of the decision but by and through the very act of God himself. The love that belongs to God is given in a profoundly personal way to the believer.

"God shows his love for us in that while we were yet sinners Christ died for us" (5:8). By this sentence, love is portrayed as the concrete event at the cross of Christ. It is not a mood or sentiment but the act of the person, Jesus Christ the Savior. In this passage Paul agrees completely with John's words, "In this is love, not that we loved God but that he loved us and sent his son to be the expiation for our sins" 1 John 4:10).

The final paragraphs in Romans 5, the two Adams narrative, are of vital importance for the development of the Apostle's definition of *agapē*. He establishes the relationship of *agapē* to the word "grace" (*charis*), "For if many died through one man's trespass, much more have the grace of God and the free gift in the grace of that one man, Jesus Christ, abounded for many" (5:15). In this text the *grace* of God in the act of one man, Christ, is equated to the earlier statement concerning the *love* of God poured into our hearts. Paul makes it clear that his use of grace, which is a word widely used and very familiar to the Greek world, is to be understood in the perspective of the New Testament word *agapē*. This means that to the Greek reader, grace is receiving its definition from the more important *agapē*.

The next use of the word *agapē* is equally impressive. "I am persuaded that neither death, nor life, nor angels, nor principalities, nor things present, nor things to come, nor height, nor depth, nor anything else in all creation, will be able to separate us from the love of God in Christ Jesus our Lord" (8:38–39). The greatness of God's love in Christ; its sovereignty over every other reality, is the teaching of this passage. Once again, *agapē* belongs to the person of God himself as part of his very character.

In the next passage Paul quotes Malachi 1:2, 3: "Jacob I loved but Esau I hated" (9:13). In this Old Testament passage, *agapē* is the love that once again belongs to the decision of God. The same is the case in 9:25 by the quotation from Hosea, "Those who were not my people I will call my people, and her who was not beloved, I will call my beloved."

"As regards election they are beloved for the sake of their forefathers" (11:28). It is God who grants belovedness. In these passages of Romans 9 and 11, the further theological thread within the definition becomes clear; that is, the connection between "worth" and *agapē*. In biblical thought, *agapē* is the source word for meaning. Other words are also drawn into Paul's love vocabulary, e.g., the word translated mercy, (11:30, 31, 32, Gal. 6:16, Eph. 2:4). This commonly used word also appears in Romans 15:9; 9:23. In chapter 12:1 still another word also translated by the RSV as "mercies" appears (a word that is also used in Col. 3:12, 2 Cor. 1:3, Phil. 2:1). The word "kindness" is used of God in 11:22. The word "welcome" from the root "take hold of," literally, "to take to yourself," is used in 14:1, 3 and 15:7. These words supplement in Romans the more common use of "grace." It appears certain that the Apostle has sparingly used *agapē* within the Romans letter in order to highlight its importance.

"Let love be genuine" (12:9), "Love one another with brotherly affection" (12:10). In these verses Paul does not use *agapē* but makes use of the Greek root *phileo* to describe the spontaneous family affection that Christians should have and experience within the community of faith.

Once again the word "beloved" appears in 12:19. Finally in the paragraph 13:8–10, *agapē* appears five times. Paul now uses *agapē* as a word for the Christian. The five uses in 13:8–10 are important.

(1) Verse 8. *Agapē* is greater as an interpersonal force than all debt-loaded communication between people. *Agapē* is freedom from debts. By this opening sentence Paul affirms the essentially positive character of *agapē*. Also, the intensely personal reference "Owe no one anything except to love one another" points up the personal experience that describes a person's perception of *agapē*. *Agapē* in chapters 1–12 is the personal experience of the Christian that is received as the wondrous gift from God. Now in this passage the Christian is set free to share love in Christ (5:1–11) and

its power (8:39) in Christ with real people in real places.

(2) Verse 8. "For he who loves his neighbors has fulfilled the law." The word "fulfilled" is the RSV translation of the Greek word *plēroma*. Paul is teaching that *agapē* fills up the law to overflowing. Love goes beyond what the Law demands, and therefore the law which always states relationship in a minimal sense is not able to keep up with God's love at work within people. Here is the cumulative fact of God's love at work within the Christian church.

(3) Verse 9. Paul quotes Leviticus 19:18, "You shall not take vengeance or bear any grudge against the sons of your own people, but you shall love your neighbor as yourself: I am the Lord." By this quotation Paul provides an Old Testament underpinning of his thesis that *agapē* is the fulfillment of the Law. The love of the neighbor is not founded upon the rejection of the self. The source for love is positive, not negative. This fact has already been established by Paul. The book began with the word "beloved"—"to all God's beloved." Paul teaches an ethic that grows out of the way of love. Therefore, he rejects any form of ethical morality which honors the neighbor by dishonoring the self. Such a view would amount to an "I am not O.K. You are O.K." relationship between people which God's love has overcome in the gospel.

The Christian owes his neighbor love; that is, the Christian cannot keep to himself the love of Jesus Christ which he found by faith. This love he must share because of its own inner force. "Something there is that doesn't love a wall, that wants it down" (Robert Frost, *Mending Wall*).

(4) Verse 10. "Love does no wrong; love is the fulfilling of the law." The emphasis within this fourth and fifth usage of *agapē* is active; love creates the decision by the Christian of good will toward the neighbor. This same active sense of love at work is the intent of a later reference in 14:15, "If your brother is being injured by what you eat, you are no longer walking in love." The Christian's confession is, "It was God's love that first found me in judgment, then set me free

from judgment through the merit of Christ's sacrifice in my behalf; now it is that very love at work within my life to set me free again in order to love my neighbor." Because of *agapē*, Christian ethics for Paul is not a heavy burden but freedom in the deepest sense.

(5) "Walking in love" toward the brother in the context of 14:13–15:3 unites *agapē* with edification (15:2), mutual upbuilding (14:19), concern for the redemption of the brother (14:15). *Agapē* is free enough to care about the fulfillment and freedom of the neighbor. This is the eschatological nature of love in the New Testament. Love is not so much a power or good will energy that in measurable amounts goes forth from the Christian to the world around him, but love is the relationship in Christ which results in a relationship with the neighbor. By means of this new relationship the Christian participates alongside of the neighbor to help him reach his own full stride in faith, hope, and love.

Section 5—13:11–14—MORALITY

13: 11)Besides this you know what hour it is, how it is full time now for you to wake from sleep. For salvation is nearer to us now than when we first believed; 12)the night is far gone, the day is at hand. Let us then cast off the works of darkness and put on the armor of light; 13)let us conduct ourselves becomingly as in the day, not in reveling and drunkenness, not in debauchery and licentiousness, not in quarreling and jealousy. 14)But put on the Lord Jesus Christ, and make no provision for the flesh, to gratify its desires.

"The night is far gone. The day is at hand." Paul's hope in Christ is the basis for his morality. His closing words in 1 Corinthians 15 have the same ring to them as these sentences, "O death, where is thy sting?" The sting of death is sin, and the power of sin is the law. But thanks be to God, who gives us the victory through our Lord Jesus Christ. Therefore, my beloved brethren, be steadfast . . ." (1 Cor.

15:55–58). Because Jesus Christ stands at the end of history, Paul desires to conform his life to that fact. His life does not face the evaporation of emptiness, but the light of day. This hope becomes the source for Paul's strategy. He wagers on hope in his world view and therefore dares to bless those who are persecutors because he is convinced of the power of light over darkness. He really believes that God's love can change the persecutor. He is perfectly willing to concede the reality of darkness in the world, and he knows of it by firsthand experience; but he refuses to overrate the forces of evil.

In the Book of Romans Paul does not closely define what he means by the reference to darkness and light, as here in 13:12. Does he intend the reader to conclude that light and darkness refer to God and Satan? Satan is named within Romans only in 16:20. "Principalities . . . powers" (8:38) may be interpreted as a reference to Satan, and is certainly what is intended by the reference in Ephesians 6:12–16, "For we are not contending against flesh and blood, but against the principalities, against the powers, against the world rulers of this present darkness, against the spiritual hosts of wickedness in the heavenly places. . . . Above all take the shield of faith with which you can quench all the flaming darts of the evil one." Satan is mentioned by name in 2 Corinthians 12, ". . . A thorn in the flesh was given me in the flesh, a messenger from Satan," and in 2 Thessalonians 2:18, ". . . we wanted to come to you—I Paul, again and again—but Satan hindered us." The Ephesian passage gives excellent basis for interpreting Paul's references in 8:38 and 13:12 as references to cosmic moral evil—the devil, Satan, the evil one. But Paul will not preoccupy himself with even such prestigious power, for "salvation is nearer to us now" (13:11). Salvation is used by Paul in this text to refer to the ultimate salvation that goes with the fulfillment of history. Romans 8:18–25 is in effect an enlargement in more detail of this single sentence. The Apostle uses "save" in a double sense. In 8:24 "saved" is used to refer to the Christian's present-tense experience, whereas in 13:11 the word points beyond the present to the future fulfillment.

In the assurance of the victory of God's light over darkness, Paul exhorts his fellow Christians to wake up to their opportunities. It is within the positive context of light that Paul teaches in specific terms about the Christian's moral style of life. Morality is not taught within the framework of warning but rather within the framework of hope. Paul's thesis is that where hope in the meaningful future is believed in the present, this conviction sets the individual free from the life styles of darkness. This means that Paul draws a basic connection between hope and morality and inversely between despair and immorality. Despair is the inevitable companion of idolatry, because the very nature of idols—the "no gods" that men set up to worship—is to rob their subjects of any break of daylight (*The Silver Chair*, C. S. Lewis). Paul plainly connects idolatry and immorality in a passage very similar to Romans 13:11–14. In Colossians 3:5, 12 he writes: "Put to death, therefore, what is earthly in you; immorality, impurity, passion, evil desire, the covetousness which is idolatry. . . . Put on then, as God's chosen ones, holy and beloved, compassion, kindness. . . ." But hope means that the Christian trusts in the greater power of the daylight. Paul, therefore, calls upon the Christians to decide upon the way of God's daylight for their own life-style here and now.

Section 6—Romans 14:1–15:13—THE CHURCH

14: 1)As for the man who is weak in faith, welcome him, but not for disputes over opinions. 2)One believes he may eat anything, while the weak man eats only vegetables. 3)Let not him who eats despise him who abstains, and let not him who abstains pass judgment on him who eats; for God has welcomed him. 4)Who are you to pass judgment on the servant of another? It is before his own master that he stands or

falls. And he will be upheld, for the Master is able to
make him stand.

5)One man esteems one day as better than another,
while another man esteems all days alike. Let every
one be fully convinced in his own mind. 6)He who
observes the day, observes it in honor of the Lord. He
also who eats, eats in honor of the Lord, since he gives
thanks to God; while he who abstains, abstains in
honor of the Lord and gives thanks to God. 7)None of
us lives to himself, and none of us dies to himself. 8)
If we live, we live to the Lord, and if we die, we die to
the Lord; so then, whether we live or whether we die,
we are the Lord's. 9)For to this end Christ died and
lived again, that he might be Lord both of the dead
and of the living.

10)Why do you pass judgment on your brother? Or
you, why do you despise your brother? For we shall all
stand before the judgment seat of God; 11)for it is
written,

"As I live, says the Lord, every knee shall bow to me,
and every tongue shall give praise to God."

12)So each of us shall give account of himself to God.

13)Then let us no more pass judgment on one another, but rather decide never to put a stumbling
block or hindrance in the way of a brother. 14)I know
and am persuaded in the Lord Jesus that nothing is
unclean in itself; but it is unclean for any one who
thinks it unclean. 15)If your brother is being injured
by what you eat, you are no longer walking in love.
Do not let what you eat cause the ruin of one for
whom Christ died. 16)So do not let what is good to
you be spoken of as evil. 17)For the kingdom of God
does not mean food and drink but righteousness and
peace and joy in the Holy Spirit; 18)he who thus
serves Christ is acceptable to God and approved by
men. 19)Let us then pursue what makes for peace and
for mutual upbuilding. 20)Do not, for the sake of
food, destroy the work of God. Everything is indeed
clean, but it is wrong for any one to make others fall
by what he eats; 21)it is right not to eat meat or
drink wine or do anything that makes your brother
stumble. 22)The faith that you have, keep between
yourself and God; happy is he who has no reason to
judge himself for what he approves. 23)But he who
has doubts is condemned, if he eats, because he does
not act from faith; for whatever does not proceed
from faith is sin.

15: 1)We who are strong ought to bear with the failings of the weak, and not to please ourselves; 2)let each of us please his neighbor for his good, to edify him. 3)For Christ did not please himself; but, as it is written, "The reproaches of those who reproached thee fell on me." 4)For whatever was written in former days was written for our instruction, that by steadfastness and by the encouragement of the scriptures we might have hope. 5)May the God of steadfastness and encouragement grant you to live in such harmony with one another, in accord with Christ Jesus, 6)that together you may with one voice glorify the God and Father of our Lord Jesus Christ.

7)Welcome one another, therefore, as Christ has welcomed you, for the glory of God. 8)For I tell you that Christ became a servant to the circumcised to show God's truthfulness, in order to confirm the promises given to the patriarchs, 9)and in order that the Gentiles might glorify God for his mercy. As it is written,
"Therefore I will praise thee among the Gentiles,
   and sing to thy name";
10)and again it is said,
"Rejoice, O Gentiles, with his people";
11)and again,
"Praise the Lord, all Gentiles,
   and let all the peoples praise him";
12)and further Isaiah says,
"The root of Jesse shall come,
he who rises to rule the Gentiles;
in him shall the Gentiles hope."
13)May the God of hope fill you with all joy and peace in believing, so that by the power of the Holy Spirit you may abound in hope.

"For the Master is able to make him stand." This is a long passage, the length of which in itself is an interesting feature of the text. The Apostle Paul feels that the health of the church is of critical importance to the mission of the gospel, and, therefore, he devotes these many sentences to the question of that health.

His method in the passage is to isolate several issues that are current in the first-century church. His reply to the issues is first to affirm two overarching facts and then to call upon the church at Rome to resolve for themselves the issues on the basis of the great facts. The first fact is found in 14:4, "Who are you to pass judgment on the servant of another? It is before his own master that he stands or falls." Paul's rhetorical question establishes the ground upon which the people of the church stand in relation to each other. Christ himself is the Lord of the church, and each member of the body stands individually before the Lord. "So each of us shall give account of himself to God" (14:12).

The Apostle then establishes a second thesis: "Let us then pursue what makes for peace and for mutual upbuilding . . . may the God of steadfastness and encouragement grant you to live in such harmony with one another, in accord with Jesus Christ, that together you may with one voice glorify the God and father of our Lord" (14:19; 15:5, 6).

If it is true that each Christian stands separately before Christ and is welcomed by him, so it is equally true that the Christian together with the whole church is to glorify the Lord alongside of his fellow disciples. The separate Christian then, without any damage done to his individual integrity, is granted solemn responsibility for the healthiness of the whole fellowship.

"As for the man who is weak in faith, welcome him but not for disputes over opinions" (14:1). Paul acknowledges that within the church there are degrees of growth in faith— from weakness to strength. He also admits to controversy within the church. The counsel of the Apostle is that variance of opinion within the church is not to be feared. "Welcome him" is the advice he gives to each reader who naturally reads the text from his own existential situation. He counsels against the polemical style of church relationship which cannot endure the difference of opinion within the church. Paul establishes two criteria for the church in this question.

(1) What is truly meant to be central must remain central; and (2) the goal for each Christian in the church is the upbuilding of his fellow Christian in what is truly central.

Paul is clear that it is the Lord who is the center for the church. His reference to the illustration of servant–master in 13:4 makes the point that all Christians are servants of the one master, and it is not the task of one Christian to pass judgment upon another Christian who enjoys his own unique relationship with the Lord. This argument is stated plainly in 14:8: "If we live, we live to the Lord, and if we die, we die to the Lord . . . we are the Lord's," and in 14:18, "He who serves Christ is acceptable." The inference in the whole passage is that conflict of opinion regarding matters other than the central question of the Lordship of Christ does not harm the church as much as does controversy that results in Christians bearing judgment toward one another. Judgment is the more serious offense because it displaces the central place of Christ as Lord. The Christian who judges his fellow Christian rather than welcoming him has placed his own criteria, whatever that criteria may be, at the center. Usually the new criteria are the distinctive view he personally holds at variance with others. Paul will not allow this to go by un-challenged, since the Christian who practices such judg-ment has in effect drawn a new circle for the church making use of his own favored view as the surrogate center for the new circle.

A diagrammatic sketch may help to portray this unfortu-nate phenomena.

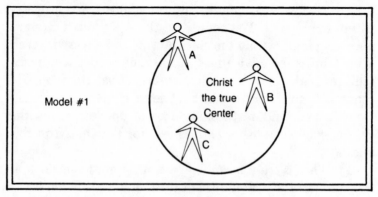

If Christian B were to successfully judge his fellow Christians A or C, he would need to absolutize his own viewpoint in order to sustain his judgment. Therefore, he must create for practical purposes a new circle:

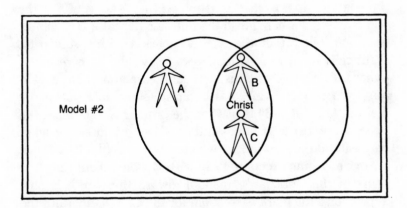

Model #2

The new circle drawn by B excludes A and perhaps includes C. Being a Christian he would include Christ, but now Christ is incorporated into the circle of B as an ingredient, but the lordship of Christ is compromised. The situation for Christian B and his followers in Model 2 is that whatever viewpoint or practice which now has taken on such all-encompassing importance for them—whether it is vegetarianism, liturgical calendars, or a hundred other possible convictions—is not the real center. Though the distinctive concern may be valid when viewed as a part of the larger whole, it does not have the substance to become central. The irony of Christian B and his followers is that they end up as people devoted to and preoccupied with concerns that would never have won them to become Christians in the first place. Only Christ is great enough to win men and women to himself. Vegetarianism, church politics, or position papers on important issues never match the appeal of Jesus of Nazareth, neither do they set free the follower from sin, death and the power of the devil.

Paul rejects Model 2. He calls for a more dynamic relationship between Christians in which within the circle of Model 1 each Christian maintains his own freedom and integrity by subjecting himself to the Lord of the circle and seeking to aid each fellow Christian in his or her own growth in relationship to what is truly central. The goal for the Christian is neither the status quo nor the false freedom of isolation, but rather the creative tension within solidarity. Paul calls upon each Christian to know and to care about what his fellow Christians know and care about. He is calling for a way of living that is sensitive and interpersonally helpful (Phil. 4:1-3). Love for the brother is, therefore, the second criterion, "If your brother is being injured by what you eat, you are no longer walking in love" (14:15). "Owe no one anything except to love" (13:8), which Paul gave as a mark of the Christian's freedom toward the world, is now repeated as the mark of freedom for the Christian within the church.

Paul challenges the stronger Christian "to bear with the failings of the weak." However, to preserve the weak from the dead-end street of having their way in all matters by virtue of weakness, the Apostle qualifies the counsel with the love criterion—love involves the participation of Christians with each other to the end that mutual upbuilding in faith, hope and love takes place. Paul thereby calls for discernment and hard work if the criterion of love is to be expressed. Love must care enough for the brother and sister to distinguish between wants and needs, must care enough to bear weight. The reward that love receives is in sharing the journey to freedom on the part of another human being. As the neighbor discovers his own full stride as a Christian, then love has its reward. This final note is the intent of Paul's compended quotation of Psalm 18:49, 2 Samuel 22:50, Deuteronomy 32:43, Psalm 117:1, and Isaiah 11:10 (15:9-12).

Section 7—Romans 15:14–33—PRAYER

15: 14)I myself am satisfied about you, my brethren, that you yourselves are full of goodness, filled with all knowledge, and able to instruct one another. 15)But on some points I have written to you very boldly by way of reminder, because of the grace given me by God 16)to be a minister of Christ Jesus to the Gentiles in the priestly service of the gospel of God, so that the offering of the Gentiles may be acceptable, sanctified by the Holy Spirit. 17)In Christ Jesus, then, I have reason to be proud of my work for God. 18)For I will not venture to speak of anything except what Christ has wrought through me to win obedience from the Gentiles, by word and deed, 19)by the power of signs and wonders, by the power of the Holy Spirit, so that from Jerusalem and as far round as Illyricum I have fully preached the gospel of Christ, 20)thus making it my ambition to preach the gospel, not where Christ has already been named, lest I build on another man's foundation, 21)but as it is written, "They shall see who have never been told of him, and they shall understand who have never heard of him."

22)This is the reason why I have so often been hindered from coming to you. 23)But now, since I no longer have any room for work in these regions, and since I have longed for many years to come to you, 24)I hope to see you in passing as I go to Spain, and to be sped on my journey there by you, once I have enjoyed your company for a little. 25)At present, however, I am going to Jerusalem with aid for the saints. 26)For Macedonia and Achaia have been pleased to make some contribution for the poor among the saints at Jerusalem; 27)they were pleased to do it, and indeed they are in debt to them, for if the Gentiles have come to share in their spiritual blessings, they ought also to be of service to them in material blessings.

28)When, therefore, I have completed this, and have delivered to them what has been raised, I shall go on by way of you to Spain; 29)and I know that when I come to you I shall come in the fulness of the blessing of Christ. 30)I appeal to you, brethren, by our Lord Jesus Christ and by the love of the Spirit, to strive together with me in your prayers to God on my behalf, 31)that I may be delivered from the unbelievers in Judea, and that my service for Jerusalem may be acceptable to the saints, 32)so that by God's

will I may come to you with joy and be refreshed in
your company. 33)The God of peace be with you all
Amen.

"Strive together with me in your prayers." The sentence of
15:13 has the sound of a closing greeting, and 15:14 may be
the point where Paul takes the pen into his own hand to
write his final personal note to the letter. It is Paul's practice
to dictate the letter to a scribe (*amanuesis*, Rom. 16:22),
and then to write in his own hand the final few sentences
(note Gal. 6:11, 2 Cor. 16:21; Col. 4:18; 2 Thess. 3:17).

These sentences are personal. He explains the purpose of
the letter, "On some points I have written to you very boldly
by way of reminder" (16:15). The Christians who receive
the letter are in Christ because of the gospel, and Paul has
sought to state the sweeping groundwork and implications
of that gospel in order that they might grow in faith, "so
that the offering of the Gentiles may be acceptable, sanctified by the Holy Spirit."

Paul surveys his own ministry with its successes. "In Christ
Jesus, then, I have reason to be proud of my work for God
. . . by word and deed, by the power of signs and wonders,
by the power of the Holy Spirit. . . ." (15:17–29). Paul
certainly cannot be accused of being self-depreciative and
mouselike; he shows signs of considerable ego strength in
every letter. He is never hesitant to use the first person
singular or to tell frankly what are his own feelings. This
total lack of evasiveness by Paul reveals his thought and
personality much more fully than is the case of those New
Testament writers who write more cautiously. The sharpest
contrast in this regard exists between the letters of Paul and
the Johannine literature. Paul writes like Jeremiah or David;
John writes like Isaiah.

Within the context of this personal account of journeys
and proposed missions, the Apostle asks for the prayers of
the Roman Christians: "I appeal to you, brethren, by our

Lord Jesus Christ and by the love of the Spirit, to strive together with me in your prayers to God on my behalf" (15: 30).

At this point we want to consider Paul's doctrine of prayer as it has surfaced within this letter to the Romans. There are four direct references to prayer here. The first (1:8–12) contains Paul's statement of his own prayer for the Romans, "Without ceasing I mention you always in my prayers, asking . . ." (1:9).

Secondly, note his discussion of prayer in chapter 8, "Likewise the Spirit helps us in our weakness, for we do not know how to pray as we ought, but the Spirit himself intercedes for us with sighs too deep for words" (8:26, 27).

In the 12th chapter he exhorts the people to pray, "Rejoice in your hope, be patient in tribulation, be constant in prayer" (12:12).

What we have within the Romans letter is not in any sense a complete teaching by the Apostle regarding prayer, but rather these four direct references to prayer and some other indirect references: regarding Abraham, "He grew strong in his faith as he gave glory to God" (4:20); "But how are men to call upon him? . . ." (10:14). An oblique third person prayer is recorded in 11:33–36: "O the depth of the riches." Paul uses a quotation from Isaiah 45:23 in 14:11. ". . . every tongue shall give praise. . . ." The last one is in 15:6: ". . . together you may with one voice glorify the God and father of our Lord Jesus Christ."

The doctrine on the basis of Paul's direct and indirect statements in Romans takes the following shape.

(1) Prayer describes the relationship of men and women speaking to God. It is the bringing of the whole self to the Lord (12:1).

(2) Prayer is seen as intercession to God on behalf of other people (1:9, 15:30).

(3) Prayer is portrayed as the *cry for help* for the one who prays (1:10, 10:14, 15:30, 8:26).

(4) Prayer is man praising and thanking God (1:8, 4:20, 11:33, 12:12, 15:6, 15:30, 14:11, 15:9–12).

(5) Prayer is seen as a regular experience of the Christian (1:9, 12:12).

(6) Prayer is portrayed as the experience within which the Christian must continually grow and learn by help from the Holy Spirit (8:26–27).

(7) Prayer is portrayed as an individual and a community experience (1:8–10, 15:30) "I mention," "strive with me."

(8) Prayer is treated with great earnestness by Paul. Prayer was a regular part of his life.

The most important fact to note about prayer within Romans and, indeed, in the whole of the biblical witness, is that prayer is never seen as bargaining with God. The root word for pray (evoke) in Classical Greek carries with it the connotation of pledge or solemn vow made by a man or woman to the deities in return for favors and special blessings he might grant. Within the biblical teaching on prayer, this sense of bargaining is simply not present. Note the Romans references again with this awareness. One is deeply impressed by the presence of a totally new kind of prayer from what the secular world knew.

C. S. Lewis in *The Magician's Nephew* wonderfully captures this fact in the scene between Diggory and Aslan. Diggory is tempted to bargain with Aslan, hoping to win help for his mother, who is critically ill, in return for a brave deed. But before Diggory speaks his bargain, he sees the massive paw of the Lion with its claws; he realizes that Aslan is not one with whom he should bargain. So, he submits to Aslan's authority and agrees to go on the long mission. Then, in that context, he blurts out: "O Aslan, could you please help my mother!" This is prayer in biblical faith. Submitting to the authority of Jesus Christ as Lord and having discovered not only his power but his love, we cry out for help—and anything goes. It's a relationship.

Section 8—Romans 16:1–27—THE NAMES

16: 1)I commend to you our sister Phoebe, a deconess of the church at Cenchreae, 2)that you may receive her in the Lord as befits the saints, and help her in whatever she may require from you, for she has been a helper of many and of myself as well. 3)Greet Prisca and Aquila, my fellow workers in Christ Jesus, 4)who risked their necks for my life, to whom not only I but also all the churches of the Gentiles give thanks; 5)greet also the church in their house. Greet my beloved Epaenetus, who was the first convert in Asia for Christ. 6)Greet Mary, who has worked hard among you. 7)Greet Andronicus and Junias, my kinsmen and my fellow prisoners; they are men of note among the apostles, and they were in Christ before me. 8)Greet Ampliatus, my beloved in the Lord. Greet Urbanus, our fellow worker in Christ, and my beloved Stachys.

10)Greet Apelles, who is approved in Christ. Greet those who belong to the family of Aristobulus. 11)Greet my kinsman Herodion. Greet those in the Lord who belong to the family of Narcissus. 12)Greet those workers in the Lord, Tryphaena and Tryphosa. Greet the beloved Persis, who has worked hard in the Lord. 13)Greet Rufus, eminent in the Lord, also his mother and mine. 14)Greet Asyncritus, Phlegon, Hermes, Patrobas, Hermas, and the brethren who are with them. 15)Greet Philologus, Julia, Nereus and his sister, and Olympas, and all the saints who are with them.

16)Greet one another with a holy kiss. All the churches of Christ greet you. 17)I appeal to you, brethren, to take note of those who create dissensions and difficulties, in opposition to the doctrine which you have been taught; avoid them. 18)For such persons do not serve our Lord Christ, but their own appetites, and by fair and flattering words they deceive the hearts of the simple-minded. 19)For while your obedience is known to all, so that I rejoice over you, I would have you wise as to what is good and guileless as to what is evil; 20)then the God of peace will soon crush Satan under your feet. The grace of our Lord Jesus Christ be with you. 21)Timothy, my fellow worker, greets you; so do Lucius and Jason and Sosipater, my kinsmen. 22)I Tertius, the writer of this

letter, greet you in the Lord. 23)Gaius, who is host to
me and to the whole church, greets you, Erastus, the
city treasurer, and our brother Quartus, greet you.
25)Now to him who is able to strengthen you according to my gospel and the preaching of Jesus Christ,
according to the revelation of the mystery which was
kept secret for long ages 26)but is now disclosed and
through the prophetic writings is made known to all
nations, according to the command of the eternal
God, to bring about the obedience of faith—27)to the
only wise God be glory for evermore through Jesus
Christ! Amen.

"Greet Prisca and Aquila." Some interpreters have speculated that this final chapter is either an addendum to the
book which formally concluded with chapter 15 or that
chapter 16 may in fact be a letter to another church, such as
Ephesus, which was attached somehow to the Romans letter.
The second proposal is made because of the presence of the
long list of names. It is argued that Paul would not possibly
know so many people at Rome, in view of the fact that he
had not actually visited there.

The most compelling conclusion, with all of the evidence
before us, however, is to interpret chapter 16 as it stands—
a witness to the interest of Paul in people. He knows their
names; he desires to honor them; he wants the Christian
community at Rome to share his appreciation for these
friends. As Anders Nygren has noted, the length of the
list of names is all the more conclusive evidence that the
greeting is meant for Rome. Since Paul knew virtually all of
the Christians at Ephesus, it is unlikely that he would list
some two dozen for special mention, thus ignoring the
others. Whereas, the list makes perfect sense when addressed
to the church he has not visited.

The list of names is of historical interest, in that it demonstrates the mobility of the Christian community within the
first century. The names bear curious bits of evidence concerning the wide and colorful ministry of Paul, also the list
shows how broadly based the Christian church is in its

membership. Perhaps one of the most interesting facts about Romans 16 is the number of women who are listed, and in prominent places. A woman Phoebe carries the letter. Prisca is mentioned before Aquila. It is clear that for Paul the Lordship of Christ has set free Greek and Jew, male and female, to be and become all that God intends them to be. Where the lists of gifts appear they are not limited either by racial origin or by sex. The wondrous freedom from old patterns and captivities is one of the marks of the Christian community and this list of names in chapter 16 is an incredible testimony to the universal relevance of Jesus Christ. Consider just a few of the names and some of the speculations we are able to make concerning these names.

Paul greets two fellow prisoners, perhaps men whom he had won to Christ while he himself was imprisoned.

He honors the prominent couple Prisca and Aquila, formerly of Ephesus and now at Rome.

The list is international. He greets Persis—literally, the "Persian woman"; Epaenetus, the first convert in Asia Minor; Rufus, literally, the "red one." Is this the Rufus mentioned in Mark 15:21, the son of Simon of Cyrene?

He greets prominent citizens. Aristobulus could have been the wealthy brother of Herod Agrippa I.

He greets common people. Hermes is a common name given to slaves and rarely given to free men. The reference to those of the house of Narcissus could also be slaves. There is Appelles—could he be the actor mentioned in an ancient inscription?

Lucius is mentioned among the group with Paul. This may be Luke.

Tertius introduces himself as the *amanuesis*, the secretary of Paul.

In verse 17 the Apostle expresses his opposition for those who "create dissensions." It is not clear what is the teaching or emphasis of these persons. Does false teaching relate to the dietary or day observance problems of chapter 14 and

15? Or perhaps it is of the style of the Corinthian "parties" factionalism? Or is it an incipient Gnostic group which is dividing the church? Paul cuts the warning short in verse 19 as he shares his confidence in God's grace at work within the fellowship at Rome. He is optimistic of victory. Paul's affirmation of victory is not spoken in the obscure language of the distant future but in the immediate experience of their Christian journey here and now. He promises that "the God of peace will soon crush Satan under your feet" (16:20).

The letter closes as it began, with an overview of the gospel stated in abrupt, sparse sentences. Paul may once again be informally quoting an apostolic church credal statement, as is very likely the case in 1:3–5, 3:24, 25, 10:9, and 10.

As Paul had started his letter, now he closes, daring to call the Romans to believe in Jesus Christ with their whole lives. The same phrase "obedience of faith" appears here as appeared in 1:5. It is not enough to hear the gospel of Jesus Christ or to study its rich meaning; but the man and woman who hears must obey the gospel and the gospel's Lord.

"We demand faith, no more and no less . . . we do not demand belief in our faith . . . we demand faith in Jesus. . . . For all faith is both simple and difficult, for all alike it is a scandal . . . and it is possible for all, only because for all it is equally impossible."[12]

Unless God himself authenticates the gospel to our hearts and minds, it is impossible to believe in Christ. But we thank God that the gospel does make sense, because God himself confirms Jesus Christ to us uniquely. And so we believe, the strengthening of his grace by the Holy Spirit continues throughout our lives. Through ups and downs the Lord is faithful. Paul ends the letter with the Hebrew word for faithful, *Amen*—literally, fixed, reliable. God is the Rock. He is faithful. Paul's letter is good news because the sixteen chapters have called upon each of us to do only one thing— to believe in God's faithfulness. Amen.

NOTES

INTRODUCTION

1. Bruce M. Metzger, *The New Testament: Its Background, Growth and Content* (Nashville: Abingdon, 1965), p. 229.
2. Günther Bornkamm argues for the early church origin of chapters 1:2–4. He sees Paul's statement in 1:16, 17 as the apostle's commentary upon the credal formula. G. Bornkamm, *Paul* (London: Hodder & Stoughton, 1969), p. 248. A. M. Hunter argues that 3:24, 25 and 10:8, 9, as well as 1:2–4, are also credal formulas. A. M. Hunter, *Paul and his Predecessors* (London: SCM, 1961), pp. 120–122.

PART I

1. C. H. Dodd, *The Epistle to the Romans* (London: Hodder & Stoughton, 1949), p. 5.
2. Gerhard Kittel and Gerhard Friedrich, *Theological Dictionary of the New Testament*, Geoffrey W. Bromiley (tr.), Volume V (Grand Rapids: Eerdmans, 1967), p. 453.

PART II

1. Ernst Käsemann, *New Testament Questions Today* (London: SCM, 1969), p. 57.
2. The phrase "righteousness of God" is rich in its Hebraic sources. It appears in Deut. 33:21, translated in RSV as "the just decrees of the Lord" (James 1:20; Matt. 6:33; and even in Rule of Qumran 11:12). Paul is not using righteousness as a statis attribute of God but as the awesome decision of the trustworthy God at work toward men.
3. Paul's wording of Habakkuk 2:4 (a favorite of his Old Testament quotations, also quoted it in Galatians 3:11) is from the Septuagint text of the Old Testament. This Habakkuk quotation, like the phrase "righteousness of God," held strong sway with other first-century Jewish groups. It is quoted in *The Hymns of the Initiates* (Dead Sea Scrolls),

and in the Talmud (TB Makkoth 24A, where it is made the resolution for the Amos 5:4 command).

4. Bo Reicke, *New Testament Era, 500 BC to 100 AD* (London: Adam & Chas. Black, 1969). By 67 A.D., Reicke estimates that there were some 40,000 Christians in the Mediterranean world. By 100 A.D. he estimates 80,000 in Asia Minor alone. "Perhaps this figure appears surprising, but if anything, it is probably too low . . . on the basis of these calculations, each of which gives the probable minimum for the church as a whole about 100 A.D., we arrive at a total of more than 320,000 believers and adherents" (p. 304).

5. H. Bettenson, *Documents of the Christian Church* (Oxford: Oxford University Press, 1943), p. 5.

6. Malcolm Muggeridge, lecture delivered at Regent College, Vancouver, Canada.

7. I mean by incipient Gnostic or Protognostic the attempt to capture Christ and remake him as a redeemer force to be safely incorporated into a basically platonic world view so that redemption means really escape from the material and Christ is reduced to "a redemption ideal" or redeemed redeemer.

PART III

1. Ernst Käsemann, *New Testament Questions of Today* (Philadelphia: Fortress), p. 177.

2. C. K. Barrett, *A Commentary on the Epistle to the Romans* (London: Adams & Chas. Black, 1957). Dr. Barrett rejects the various attempts by some interpreters to see 1:18–3:20 as a digression in the book. Günther Bornkamm, *Early Christian Experiences* (London: SCM, 1969), p. 47, also insists upon the integral positioning of 1:18–3:20 and notes the deliberate parallelism Paul constructs between 1:16 and 1:18—"the righteousness of God is revealed. . . ." "The wrath of God is revealed."

3. Bornkamm, *Early Christian Experiences*, p. 59.

4. Karl Barth, *The Epistle to the Romans* (London: Oxford University Press, 1933), p. 50.

5. See further discussion in J. B. Lightfoot, *Notes on Epistles of St. Paul* (London: Macmillan, 1895), p. 254.

6. The date is the estimate of Wm. Deane, Oxford scholar of the first-century period in his book, *Book of Wisdom, Greek Text, Latin Vulgate, Authorized English Text and a Commentary* (London: Oxford University Press, 1881), pp. 82–86.

7. 2 Cor. 6:9 is the only other reference to homosexuality.

8. Karl Barth, *Epistle to the Romans* (London: Oxford University Press), p. 51.

9. Lightfoot, *Notes on the Epistle of St. Paul*, p. 254.

10. John Calvin, *Commentary on Epistle of Paul to the Romans* (Grand Rapids: Eerdmans, 1947), p. 36.

11. Martin Luther, *Lectures on Romans* (St. Louis: Concordia Press, 1972) 25:12.

12. Dietrich Bonhoeffer, *Letters and Papers from Prison* (New York: Macmillan, Fontana Books, 1959), p. 50.

13. Wolfhart Pannenberg, *Jesus-God and Man* (London: SCM, 1968), p. 262.

PART IV

1. F. F. Bruce, The Epistle of Paul to the Romans (Tyndale N.T. Commentaries), London: Tyndale Press, 1963.

2. Ibid, p. 106.

3. Otto Piper, *New Testament Lexicography*, Festschrift for E. W. Gingrich (Leiden: E. J. Brill, 1972), p. 202.

4. Joachim Jeremias, *Central Message of the New Testament* (London: Scot, 1965), p. 55.

5. Karl Barth, *Dogmatics in Outline* (New York: Harper & Row, 1956), p. 42.

6. Karl Barth, *Epistle to the Romans* (London: Oxford University Press), pp. 165, 166. John Murray, *Epistle of Paul to the Romans* (Grand Rapids: Eerdmans, 1960), in Appendix D writes an exegetical critique of Barth's treatment of chapter 5. Unfortunately though many of Murray's comments are excellent he fails to grapple with Barth's dialectical approach, and Murray avoids noting Barth's own insistence upon

the "critical moment" by which Barth interprets the essential importance of decision on the part of man.

PART V

1. Rudolph Bultmann, *Primitive Christianity in its Contemporary Setting*, translated by R. H. Fuller (New York: Meridian Books, 1956), p. 177.

2. James H. Robinson and Helmut Kooster, *Trajectories through Early Christianity* (Philadelphia: Fortress, 1971), pp. 14, 15.

3. Raymond E. Brown, *Gospel According to John One to Twelve* Anchor Bible, No. 29 (New York: Doubleday, 1973), p. IV.

4. Edwin M. Yamauchi, *Pre-Christian Gnosticism* (London: Tyndale, 1973), p. 165.

5. R. McL. Wilson, *New Testament Studies* (Cambridge: University Press, 1971), p. 70.

6. Martin Dibelius, *Paul* (London: Longmans Green & Co., 1953), p. 108.

7. Barth, p. 203.

8. See Gerhard Kittel and Gerhad Friedrich, *Theological Dictionary of the New Testament*, Vol. I (Grand Rapids: Eerdmans, 1967), p. 35.

9. J. A. Beet, *Commentary on the Epistle to Romans* (London: Hodder & Stoughton, 1886), p. 220.

10. Bultmann, *Primitive Christianity in its Contemporary Setting*, p. 287.

11. Kenneth S. Wuest, *Romans in the Greek New Testament* (Grand Rapids: Eerdmans, 1956), p. 91.

12. Anders Nygren, *Commentary on Romans* (London: SCM Press, 1952), p. 295.

13. Bruce, p. 151.

14. Calvin, *Commentary on Epistle of Paul to the Romans*, p. 262.

15. Both Calvin and Luther quote extensively from St. Augustine in supporting their interpretations.

16. Luther, *Lectures on Romans*, p. 336.

17. Barth, *Commentary on Romans,* pp. 260, 261.

18. Bruce, p. 41.

19. Käsemann, *New Testament Questions Today,* p. 13.

20. Rudolph Bultmann and F. Miller, have argued that several verses in chapter 8 are glosses (later additions to Paul's original text). In their view these include 7:24, 25, 8:2, 10, 11, 13, 15A, 17. Their arguments are not supported by mss. evidence and therefore we stay with the RSV text.

21. Some ancient mss. read in 8:2: "For the Law of the Spirit of life in Christ Jesus has set *you* free." NEB makes use of this variant in its textual reading.

22. Jürgen Moltmann, *Interpretation* 1972 "The 'Crucified God' a Trinitarian Theology of the Cross." "We have interpreted the cross in a Trinitarian manner as an event occurring in the relationship between persons. . . ." Moltmann is attempting to understand the mystery within the sentence "God so loved the world that he gave his only son" (John 3:16), and in Romans 8, "God spared not his own son. . . ."

23. F. F. Bruce, p. 163.

24. John Calvin, *Institutes of the Christian Religion,* John T. McNeill, ed. (Philadelphia: Westminster).

25. John Calvin, *Commentary on Epistle of Paul to the Romans,* p. 299.

26. Martin Luther, *Lectures on Romans,* p. 350.

27. Robert M. Grant, *A Historical Introduction to the New Testament* (London: Collins, 1963), p. 202.

28. Karl Barth, *Dogmatics in Outline* (New York: Harper & Row, 1959), p. 62.

29. C. H. Dodd, *New Testament Studies* (New York: Scribner's, 1952), p. 144.

30. Dietrich Bonhoeffer, *Letters and Papers from Prison* (London: SCM Press, 1953), p. 135.

PART VI

1. John Calvin, *Commentary on Epistle of Paul to the Romans,* p. 443.

2. The actual text in 28:16 does not include the idea of

stumbling. However, Paul combines the 28:13 reference to stumbling with Isa. 8:14 into verse 16. This is his interpretation of the whole contextual meaning of Isaiah's teaching.

3. A system of doctrine taught in the C. I. Scofield notes to the Bible, L. S. Chafer, H. Lindsay *The Late Great Planet Earth*. A helpful and scholarly study of the whole subject of prophecy from the New Testament theological standpoint, including discussion of the dangers in dispensationalism, is found in Professor G. C. Berkouwer's book *The Return of Christ*, tr. J. Van Oosterom (Grand Rapids: Wm. B. Eerdmans, 1972). Also see the work of L. Berkhof, *Reformed Dogmatics* (Grand Rapids: Wm. B. Eerdmans, 1932) 2:336 ff. Berkhof challenges the overweighting of Rev. 20:1-6 by dispensational prophetic interprets. He points out, "Sound exegesis certainly requires that the obscure passages of scripture be read in the light of the clearer ones, and not vice versa" (p. 336).

4. F. F. Bruce, p. 221.

5. Berkouwer, *The Return of Christ*, p. 339.

6. Ibid., p. 347.

7. F. F. Bruce, p. 221.

8. Karl Barth, p. 421.

PART VII

1. Anders Nygren, *Commentary on Romans*, p. 241.

2. Rudolph Bultmann, *Primitive Christianity in its Contemporary Setting*, tr. R. H. Fuller (London: Thames and Hudson, 1956), p. 188.

3. Ernst Käsemann, *New Testament Questions Today*, p. 37.

4. Barth, *Commentary on Romans*, p. 466.

5. Lightfoot, *Commentary to the Philippians*, p. 9.

6. Martin Luther, *Lectures on Romans*, p. 466.

7. Rudolph Bultmann, *Primitive Christianity in its Contemporary Setting*, p. 186.

8. Karl Barth, *Commentary on Romans*, pp. 429, 430.

9. Oscar Cullmann, *The Early Church* (London: SCM, 1956), pp. 197, 198.

10. Luther, *Lectures on Romans*, p. 466.

11. Gottfried Quell and E. Stauffer, *Bible Key Words*, tr. J. R. Coates (London: A. & C. Black, 1949), pp. 28, 30, on *agape*. "Its etymological origin is unknown. Its meaning is colourless and indefinite . . . it is striking that there is hardly any occurrence of the noun *agape* in pre-biblical Greek."

12. Karl Barth, *Commentary on Romans*, p. 99.

STUDY-DISCUSSION GUIDE TO THE COMMENTARY ON ROMANS

Here are twenty-two sets of questions intended to assist those of you who are studying the Book of Romans on your own or in small groups. I hope the questions are helpful in opening up the text for your reflection. They may also stir up other questions from your own standpoint.

In addition to the questions, I will also make a few resource suggestions for those who wish to work at more depth in some particular text.

Raising the right question is at the very core of thoughtful Bible study. The five "W" questions will always be the initial step in inductive research—*who, what, where, when, why*. The questions I suggest in the guide will seek to follow up on these five "W" inductive questions.

From time to time I also suggest literary sources or images which I feel will provide windows into the great themes of the Apostle Paul.

An essential part of Bible study is to look at the words themselves as they are used in the text. For technical terms look at a *Dictionary of the Bible* (Hastings, Inter-Varsity, Interpreter's). For important theological words, the most authoritative study is the nine-volume *Theological Dictionary of the New Testament.* Other less technical books are Alan Richardson, *A Theological Word Book of the New Testament* and *A Companion to the Bible,* H. H. Rowley, Van Allmen.

1. Romans 1:1–7—The Greeting of Paul

A. SUGGESTED QUESTIONS

(1) What if you were a first-century CIA Agent with the External Affairs Section in Rome. An Agent has found a fragment of papyrus containing only the sentences of Rom. 1:1–7. On the basis of these few sentences, and only these,

describe the movement that produced them. From these sentences what do you know about these people?

(2) Compare verses 2–5 with Peter's sermon in Acts 2. Does the comparison trigger any thoughts for you?

(3) Paul uses two words, *grace* and *peace*. These words will mean different things to different people. What do they mean to you? Can you imagine what they would mean to a first-century person?

B. RESOURCES: see C. H. Dodd, *Commentary on Romans,* for his thoughts on Paul's quotation from his fellow first-century Christians. Alan Richardson, TDNT, on the particular words in the text.

2. Romans 1:8–15—Paul's Prayer

A. SUGGESTED QUESTIONS

(1) On the basis of these verses, draw up some of your own preliminary conclusions about Paul's understanding of the word *pray.*

(2) What do you make of Paul's stated feeling of debt to both the Greek-speaking and nonGreek-speaking world? Is it possible that some of his own community of faith would disagree with Paul about this? If so, why? Can you sense an issue beneath the surface, between the lines, upon which Paul now touches?

B. RESOURCES: Paul's universal vision expressed here has a parallel statement in his brief and explosive book *Galatians.* Sir Wm. Ramsay wrote on the journeys of Paul. See also James Stewart's *A Man in Christ* to understand Paul's motivation. A literary resource on the rugged figure of Paul himself is John A. Mackay's *God's Order.*

3. Romans 1:16, 17—The Manifesto of Paul

A. SUGGESTED QUESTIONS

(1) Assume for a moment that these two verses were a manifesto or preamble for his whole letter. What great

subjects, themes, questions, do you find posed here by Paul?
(2) What are his affirmations in these two verses?
(3) What issues has Paul raised for you in this manifesto? What do you now want to ask of him? What points in his statement do you want clarified, expanded?
(4) Why should he quote an Old Testament prophet?

B. RESOURCES: Word studies on *ashamed, righteousness, revealed, faith,* are very helpful here—see TDNT.

C. LITERARY RESOURCES: The universal relevance of the Christian gospel is affirmed by Paul. On this subject read D. T. Niles, *Stone of Stumbling.* Also Malcolm Muggeridge, *Jesus Rediscovered;* Blaise Pascal, *Pensées.*

4. Romans 1:18–32—The Beginning of the Prosecution Argument

A. SUGGESTED QUESTIONS
(1) Why does Paul begin his case for Christian hope on such negative ground?
(2) What do you make of Paul's view of man?
(3) React and/or respond to Paul's "exchange" concept and the portrayal of idolatry.
(4) Why the reference to homosexuality?
(5) Why the long list of sins?

B. RESOURCES: Karl Barth's discussion in his *Commentary* on this passage offers some profound explanations of Paul's heavy-handed beginning to Romans.

C. LITERARY RESOURCES abound with devastating analysis of the human crises. See T. S. Eliot, *The Love Song of J. Alfred Prufrock, Waste Land, The Cocktail Party.* For literary insight into the downward spiral of human sinfulness, see Golding's *Lord of the Flies.* K. Menninger's *Whatever Happened to Sin* discusses Western man's reluctance to face up to sin. For a remarkable insight at the dynamics of idolatry and the liberation from idols, see *The Silver Chair,* also *Magician's Nephew,* by C. S. Lewis.

5. Romans 2:1–29—The Crisis Portrayal Broadens

A. SUGGESTED QUESTIONS

(1) In chapter 1 Paul makes use of the pronoun "they." Now in chapter 2, the pronoun "you." What is your reaction to the shift in pronouns?

(2) Think for a moment of his argument. What exactly do you feel are the points he is making in chapter 2?

B. RESOURCES: See F. F. Bruce's discussion of chapter 2; also Bornkamm's *Paul.*

LITERARY RESOURCES: C. S. Lewis, *Mere Christianity* develops Paul's moral argument in a fascinating way. See the opening chapters of Lewis' book. See also the dialogue between Dr. O'Reilly and Edward in T. S. Eliot's *Cocktail Party.*

6. Romans 3:1–20—The Law Rightly Understood

A. SUGGESTED QUESTIONS

(1) What do you make of Paul's explanation of the Old Testament Law? What points does he make?

(2) What has Paul said about his own people Israel?

B. RESOURCES: To understand Paul's teaching on Israel you especially need to read Galatians, Philippians 3, 2 Corinthians. See also Karl Barth on this passage.

C. LITERARY RESOURCES: Reading *Josephus,* and *Wisdom of Solomon,* will help the student to begin to understand the Israel of the first century.

7. Romans 3:21–31—The Radical Breakthrough

A. SUGGESTED QUESTIONS

(1) What are the words Paul uses to express his case for hope?

(2) Why not try drawing your own line to express what you feel Paul is teaching in this passage.

B. RESOURCES: F. F. Bruce has a very helpful discussion of the word images of this passage.

C. LITERARY RESOURCES: Francis Thompson's *Hound of Heaven* captures something of the incredible and wondrous search and finding of mankind. See also *Lion, Witch & Wardrobe*, C. S. Lewis, for a literary portrayal of atonement. Also, Dostoyevsky's *Crime and Punishment*.

8. Romans 4:1–25—Abraham

A. SUGGESTED QUESTIONS
(1) It will be helpful to note the other references to Abraham by Paul (see Galatians). Note also the writer to the Hebrews and the references to Abraham there. Compare and contrast.
(2) Why do you think Paul brings up the name of Abraham in his book?
(3) What are the points that he makes?

B. RESOURCES: It will be very helpful for the student at this point to work through thoughtful discussions of Israel for Old Testament theology and New Testament fulfillment. See John Bright's *Kingdom of God*.

C. LITERARY RESOURCES: In the arts there just isn't a portrayal of the Mt. Moriah incident as moving and profound in my view as Rembrandt's painting *Sacrifice of Issac*.

9. Romans 5:1–11—The Love of God

A. SUGGESTED QUESTIONS
(1) Does Paul's list of human experiences and responses intrigue you (verses 3–5)?
(2) The word *agapē* appears for the first time in Ro-

mans in this text. How would you, on the basis of this text and its setting, define *agapē?* What are some of the dynamics of the word present here?

(3) On the basis of this passage, do you find clues to Paul's intent and purpose in the harsh negative beginning of Romans found in 1:18–3:20?

B. RESOURCES: The word study on *agape* in TDNT is superb. Also at this point the reader will want to read theologically on the New Testament Theology of the cross. See Baillie, *God Was in Christ,* John Stott, *Basic Christianity.*

C. LITERARY RESOURCES: What is love? Here is a theme more discussed than any other in literature, art, and music. Dostoyevsky's Sonia of *Crime and Punishment* shows us the wholeness of *agape*—both its judgment and healing. Every meeting with Aslan in *Chronicles* reveals the wonderfully subtle insight of C. S. Lewis into New Testament love. The majestic simplicity of New Testament love amazes us in the character Alyosha both in *Brothers Karamazov* and Solzhenitsyn's *One Day in the Life of Ivan Denisovich,* which is modeled after *Brothers Karamazov.* The mixture of strength and freedom is portrayed by Rembrandt's *Return of the Prodigal* in the hands of the father.

10. Romans 5:11–21—Two Adams

A. SUGGESTED QUESTIONS

(1) For a moment consider the possibility that Paul may be regathering everything that has been said so far in the book. He does this regathering with the model about the first Adam and second Adam. If that is so, what themes do you find in this summary?

(2) Why should Paul describe Jesus Christ with such an unimpressive term as Adam?

(3) Explain Paul's understanding of the purpose of the Law.

B. RESOURCES: Karl Barth's discussion in chapter 5 is a complex but very important interpretation.

C. LITERARY RESOURCES: W. H. Auden's poem *For the Time Being* portrays the significance of the identification of the divine Christ with us. See also T. S. Eliot's poem, *Journey of the Magi.*

11. Romans 6: The Christian Life

A. SUGGESTED QUESTIONS
(1) It is helpful for the student to compare other uses by Paul of hypothetical questions (see Philippians). Why do you feel Paul asks the question in verse 1?
(2) Do the prepositions *from* and *to* intrigue you? Work out the completion of those prepositional phrases throughout chapter 6.
(3) Now what about the word *freedom?* How does Paul use the word and what does he mean by it?
(4) Explain Paul's meaning of the word "baptism." What do you think he means?

B. RESOURCES: Baptism is here introduced by Paul. See Oscar Cullmann, *Baptism in the New Testament.* For an excellent survey also see the United Presbyterian General Assembly Study on Baptism by Dr. David Willis. Freedom also comes into Paul's text here, though also in chapter 1, and in fact throughout Romans. Hans Küng's books *Freedom* and *Justification* are helpful here. Also John Calvin's *Institutes.*

C. LITERARY RESOURCE: One of literature's high-water mark discussions of the freedom of Jesus Christ is in the noontime dialogue between Ivan and Alyosha in *Brothers Karamozov.*

12. Romans 7—Paul's Autobiographical Statement

A. SUGGESTED QUESTIONS
(1) Why do you feel Paul becomes so personal in this chapter?
(2) What are some of your own reactions and feelings toward this chapter?
(3) What do you feel is Paul's purpose in the chapter?

B. RESOURCES: There are sharp differences of view held regarding the autobiographical statement of Paul by interpreters of equal sincerity and thoughtfulness. Read Luther's *Commentary*, and John Beet's *Commentary* for contrasting views, also Bultmann, and then Anders Nygren for a reply to Bultmann.

C. LITERARY RESOURCES: John Bunyan's *Pilgram's Progress* is a classic artistic echo of the journey expressed by Paul in Romans 6, 7, 8. A modern classic to read is *Screwtape Letters* by C. S. Lewis.

13. Romans 8:1–27—The Holy Spirit

A. SUGGESTED QUESTIONS
(1) Describe the ministry of the Holy Spirit as you see it outlined in these verses.
(2) Describe the Holy Spirit from these verses.
(3) Why does Paul use the word "mortal bodies" in verse 11?

B. RESOURCES: F. Dale Bruner's book, *A Theology of the Holy Spirit*, is a must. Also John Stott's, *Baptism and Fullness of the Holy Spirit*. For the charismatic position in Holy Spirit theology, David duPlessis' book should be noted.

14. Romans 8:28–39—If God be for us

A. SUGGESTED QUESTIONS
(1) The word *decide* (predecide) verse 29 is a very

interesting word in the text. What do you feel is the point in Paul's discussion of the decision God has made?

(2) What is the decision God has made?

(3) What are the facts upon which Paul really establishes the foundation for his hope in this passage?

B. RESOURCES: See Karl Barth's *Dogmatics in Outline* discussion of forgiveness.

C. LITERARY RESOURCES: Martin Luther's Hymn, *A Mighty Fortress,* provides a remarkable poetic commentary to the Eighth Chapter of Romans.

15. Romans 9, 10—Discontinuity

A. SUGGESTED QUESTIONS

(1) I have used the word "discontinuity" to characterize these two opening chapters of the 3-chapter section. Reflect upon that word in connection with this passage.

(2) Comment upon verses 10:9, 10 as if they were a statement of faith for the early church.

B. RESOURCES: F. F. Bruce's commentary has very helpful in understanding these three chapters, 9, 10, 11.

16. Romans 11—Surprising Promise

A. SUGGESTED QUESTIONS

(1) Sketch in for yourself the main lines of Paul's whole discussion in chapters 9, 10, and 11.

(2) What is it that Paul states will occur?

(3) Comment upon the final benediction of chapter 11.

17. Romans 12:1–2

A. SUGGESTED QUESTIONS

(1) Why does Paul use the word "bodies" in this passage?

(2) If this passage is one more example of Paul's gathering of his total argument, comment on the passage in that light.

(3) Comment on the words "conform," "transform."

B. RESOURCES: Word studies in this passage will be very helpful. See Karl Barth's commentary.

C. LITERARY RESOURCES: *Pilgrim's Progress* is a very meaningful portrayal of the growth journey that these sentences proclaim.

18. Romans 12:3–8—The Gifts

A. SUGGESTED QUESTIONS

(1) Notice the order in Paul's argument. Does the arrangement of his points in the text interest you?

(2) Why is Paul's teaching on gifts surrounded by the context we find in these verses 3–8?

(3) On the basis of these verses, sketch in your impressions of Paul's view of the church.

B. RESOURCES: See Dale Bruner's treatment of "Gifts of the Holy Spirit" in *A Theology of the Holy Spirit.*

19. Romans 12:9–21—A Strategy Unfolds

A. SUGGESTED QUESTIONS

(1) If these verses were in fact meant to be a description by Paul of the strategy of the Christians in the world, then what would you single out as the marks of this strategy?

(2) What does the phrase "coals of fire" mean? What is Paul's point?

20. Romans 13: Consider this chapter as a whole

A. SUGGESTED QUESTIONS

(1) Think of yourself as a first-century Christian con-

fronted by the harsh realities of Roman oppression, perhaps considering some form of escape from this oppression of the real world of the first century. Respond to chapter 13 in the context of these feelings.

(2) What is the reason that Paul portrays the social order in such ideal terms?

(3) Comment on the phrase "owe no one anything except . . ." What is Paul getting at?

21. Romans 14, 15

A. SUGGESTED QUESTIONS: Let me try out some impressions of Paul's themes in Romans 12–15.

(1) Chapters 12 and 13 make the point that the Christian must live his Christian life without escape and in the real world. How would you describe the concern of Paul for the Christian in verses 14, 15?

(2) What guidelines for living in relationship with fellow Christians do you find in verses 14, 15?

(3) What are some of the threats to the church that Paul seems especially concerned about in these chapters?

B. RESOURCES: C. S. Lewis' *Mere Christianity* and *Screwtape Letters* are very helpful in working through questions on the relationship of the Christian and the Church.

22. Romans 16

A. SUGGESTED QUESTIONS

(1) Read through the names and discover your own inductive insights into the nature of the Christian church at Rome. What did you observe?

(2) Paul closes the letter much in the same way as he began. Compare the closing paragraphs with the opening paragraphs of Romans. Comment on this comparison.

(3) Work up at this point your own summary of the whole book. What main points stand out the most for you?

B. RESOURCES: F. F. Bruce's commentary has very helpful data on the list of names in chapter 16.

LaVergne, TN USA
19 May 2010
183284LV00003B/1/A